The American Labor Movement, 1955–1995

Recent Titles in
Contributions in Labor Studies

The American Labor Movement, 1955–1995

WALTER GALENSON

Contributions in Labor Studies, Number 47

GREENWOOD PRESS
Westport, Connecticut • London

Library of Congress Cataloging-in-Publication Data

Galenson, Walter, 1914–
    The American labor movement, 1955–1995 / Walter Galenson.
      p.   cm.—(Contributions in labor studies, ISSN 0886-8239 ;
  no. 47)
    Includes bibliographical references (p.   ) and index.
    ISBN 0-313-29677-4 (alk. paper)
    1. Trade-unions—United States—History—20th century. 2. Trade-
unions—United States. I. Title. II. Series.
  HD6508.G275   1996
  331.88'0973'09045—dc20   95-35686

British Library Cataloguing in Publication Data is available.

Library of Congress Catalog Card Number: 95-35686
ISBN: 0-313-29677-4
ISSN: 0886-8239

First published in 1996

Greenwood Press, 88 Post Road West, Westport, CT 06881
An imprint of Greenwood Publishing Group, Inc.

Printed in the United States of America

The paper used in this book complies with the
Permanent Paper Standard issued by the National
Information Standards Organization (Z39.48–1984).

10 9 8 7 6 5 4 3 2

Contents

Tables

Preface

The American Federation of Labor (AFL) and the Congress of Industrial Organizations (CIO) consummated a merger in 1955 after many years of fruitless negotiation. The AFL, which dated back to 1886 and was the traditional central body of American labor, had become the dominant organization after twenty years of conflict. The CIO was established in 1935 under the leadership of John L. Lewis, and by 1955 was clearly in second place.

A series of events facilitated the merger. Philip Murray, who had succeeded Lewis as president of the CIO, died on November 9, 1952 and was succeeded by Walter Reuther. Two weeks later, William Green, who had been president of the AFL for twenty-seven years, also died, and was replaced by George Meany. The changing of the guard made labor unity easier to attain.

But it still took two years of intensive negotiation before the merger was brought about. Its principal architect was Arthur J. Goldberg, who was at the time general counsel of the Steelworkers Union and later became Secretary of Labor and a justice of the U.S. Supreme Court. There had been a fight for the presidency of the CIO between Reuther and Allan Haywood, the executive vice-president of the CIO. The latter had been supported by David J. McDonald, the head of the Steelworkers Union, and relationships between him and Reuther were not of the best. Indeed, it was rumored that Reuther was cool to the merger but that McDonald was prepared to move his union and its allies into the AFL with or without Reuther, which would have left the latter with a relatively small remnant of the labor movement.

The merger agreement and the constitution of the new Federation provided for a president, a secretary-treasurer, and twenty-seven vice-presidents, all of whom were to constitute an executive council. George Meany became president and William F. Schnitzler secretary-treasurer, posts they had held in the AFL.

Of the twenty-seven vice-presidents, seventeen were to be from former AFL unions and ten from the CIO. There was also provision for an executive committee of eight, the two officers, and three each from the merging parties, but the committee never played a significant role and was eventually eliminated.

Among the conditions stipulated by the CIO were the establishment of an Industrial Union Department to parallel the existing trade departments of the AFL (Building and Construction, Railway Employees, and Metal Trades); a committee on ethical practices to deal with corruption; a mechanism for adjusting jurisdictional disputes between unions; and a commitment to the elimination of racial discrimination. All these conditions, and others as well, found their way into the constitution of the new Federation. Neither side was willing to surrender its name, so the Gordian knot was cut by using both AFL and CIO, an awkward but practical solution.

The merger was a marriage of convenience rather than of love. There were major differences among the participants on economics, politics, and how unions should be governed. There was jurisdictional overlapping at every turn, and in some cases, almost exact duplication. The CIO had set up rival national unions of electrical workers, barbers, insurance workers, leather workers, packinghouse workers, paper workers, textile workers, and seamen, among others. State and city central bodies had to be consolidated. Most of these problems were eventually solved, although the legacies of the past made for a more rocky road than had been foreseen in 1955.

CHAPTER 1

Trade Union Membership

The data on trade union membership from 1955 to 1993 do not make pleasant reading for union partisans. They are shown in Table 1.1. Along with the absolute figures the so-called density ratios appear—the relationship between union membership and the labor force.

The validity of the data must be accepted with caution. The denominator of the density ratio is the nonagricultural civilian labor force, defined by the Bureau of Labor Statistics as all employed and unemployed persons in the civilian noninstitutional population. It excludes, among others, various categories of persons who are either not working or not seeking work, and are under 16 years of age. Other labor force definitions would yield different ratios, but staying with the same definition over time provides consistency.

There are also some caveats with respect to the numerator of the ratio, union membership. The Bureau's definition of labor unions has varied over time. For example, until 1968 some associations of employees were not counted as unions, while subsequently they were included. The AFL-CIO data are based on per capita payments by affiliated national unions to the Federation, and are not audited by the latter. Some unions may choose to save money by underreporting their membership, or they may hide membership decline and enhance their prestige and convention voting power by overreporting. These deficiencies are not sufficiently great to affect basic trends; the data are generally accepted as the best available indices of union size.

The first thing to note is that the relationship of AFL-CIO members to total union membership has changed little over time, from 78.3 percent in 1955 to 80.1 percent in 1993. Throughout this period the Federation has been the dominant force in the American labor movement. It has not been plagued with the

Table 1.1
Trade Union Membership in the United States, 1955–1993 (thousands)

Year	Total membership	Density ratio (percent)	AFL-CIO membership[a]	Density ratio (percent)
1955	16,127	31.8	12,622	24.9
1961	15,401	28.5	12,553	23.2
1965	18,269	30.1	12,919	20.9[b]
1971	20,711	29.1	13,177	18.5
1975	22,207	28.9	14,070	18.3
1981	20,647	22.6	13,602	14.9
1985	16,996	18.3	13,109	14.1
1991	16,568	16.1	13,923	13.5[c]
1993	16,598	15.8	13,299	12.7

[a]AFL-CIO membership data are available only for odd years.
[b]The United Automobile Workers disaffiliated from the AFL-CIO in 1968 and rejoined in 1981.
[c]The International Brotherhood of Teamsters was expelled from the AFL-CIO in 1955 and reaffiliated in 1987.
Sources: Bureau of Labor Satistics, *Handbook of Labor Statistics*, 1975, p. 105; Bureau of Labor Statistics, *Employment and Earnings*, January issues; *Statistical Abstract of the United States*, various years; AFL-CIO, 1993 Convention, *Report of the Executive Council*, p. 61.

interfederation rivalry that prevails in many countries, or that characterized the American labor scene prior to the merger.

Second, there was a 5 percent increase in absolute AFL-CIO membership from 1955 to 1993. However, the labor force was growing more rapidly, with the result that Federation density was cut almost in half. The decline was almost monotonic, with only a slight recovery in 1957. Federation membership was temporarily reduced by the defection of the Automobile Workers Union in 1968 and raised by its reaffiliation in 1981. Similarly, the Teamsters Union was expelled in 1955 and reinstated in 1987.

Within the seeming stability of total membership over this period of almost forty years, large shifts were taking place among individual unions. These are illustrated by the data in Table 1.2 showing membership of the six largest affiliates of the AFL-CIO in 1955 and 1993. Three of the largest in 1955 no longer remained in that category in 1993. However, what might be called the membership concentration ratio remained remarkably unchanged; the six largest unions in 1955 had 42.9 percent of total membership in 1955 and 44.2 percent in 1993.

A good portion of the gap between total U.S. union membership and that of the AFL-CIO was accounted for by the independent National Education Association, which had 659,000 members in 1955 and claimed 2,172,000 in 1993, which made it the largest in the country. The remainder consisted of associations

Table 1.2
Membership in the Six Largest AFL-CIO Unions, 1955 and 1993 (thousands)

Union	1955	1993
Largest in 1955		
Teamsters	1,330	1,316
Automobile Workers	1,266	771
Steelworkers	980	421
Carpenters	750	408
Machinists	627	474
Electrical Workers	460	710
Total	5,413	4,100
Percent of AFL-CIO total	42.9	
Largest in 1993		
Teamsters	1,330	1,316
State County	99	1,167
Food and Commercial	744[a]	997
Service Employees	229[b]	919
Automobile Workers	1,266	771
Electrical Workers	460	710
Total	4,128	5,900
Percent of AFL-CIO total		44.2

[a]Represents five unions that merged after 1955.
[b]Represents three unions that merged after 1955.
Source: AFL-CIO, 1993 Convention, *Report of the Executive Council*, pp. 57–61.

that engage in some form of bargaining on behalf of their members. The American Association of University Professors is an example.

The sectoral shift of union membership reflects what has been happening to the structure of the labor force. This is illustrated by Table 1.3. Particularly notable was the tremendous growth of public sector unionism from 1956 to 1993, and the decline of manufacturing as the core of the labor movement. The new public sector entrants into the union fold were spread over a number of organizations, some of which were in both the public and private sectors.

Finally, the occupational distribution of union membership in 1992 is shown in Table 1.4. Blue-collar and skilled workers were the most heavily organized, but professionals were also well represented—largely the result of the rise in government unionism. Four out of five professionals represented by bargaining organizations were employed in the public sector.

These are the bare bones of the American labor movement over the four decades since the merger. There was a parallel decline of trade unionism in the world's industrial nations, although the American unions suffered more than most. This followed a tremendous growth from the depths of the Great Depression (there were only 2.7 million members in 1933), and many of those who

Table 1.3
Trade Union Membership by Economic Sector, 1956 and 1993 (Percent of total membership)

	1956	1993
Mining	2.9	0.6
Manufacturing	48.7	21.6
Construction	11.7	5.6
Transportation and public utilities	19.3	11.6
Wholesale and retail trade	4.9	8.2
Finance, insurance, real estate	0.3	0.8
Services	6.7	9.1
Government	5.1	42.0
Agriculture	0.4	0.5
	100.0	100.0

Sources: U.S. Department of Labor, *Handbook of Labor Statistics*, 1975, p. 382; *Statistical Abstract of the United States*, 1994, p. 439.

Table 1.4
Trade Union Membership by Occupation, 1992

	Total employed (thousands)	Percent of union members
Executive, administrative, managerial	12,008	6.0
Professional specialty	14,267	21.7
Technicians and technical support	4,147	12.3
Sales occupations	11,263	5.0
Administrative support, including clerical	18,035	13.2
Service occupations	14,898	13.9
Precision production, craft, and repair	11,038	25.1
Operators, fabricators, laborers	16,206	25.8
Farming, forestry, fishing	1,825	5.0
Total	103,687	15.8

Source: Bureau of Labor Statistics, *Employment and Earnings*, January 1993, tables 57–58.

led the upward march were still in office when decline set in. They and their successors were fully aware of what was happening and tried to stem the downward tide. The story of why they were unable to do so will unfold in the pages ahead.

CHAPTER 2

The First Five Years

Combining two labor federations that had been at loggerheads for almost two decades was no easy task. Many of the older AFL unions had been in existence for more than half a century and had strong and often rigid views on how a union should operate. Most of the CIO unions, including the two giants, the Steelworkers and the Automobile Workers, had been formed in the mid-1930s or later, and tended to be more liberal. Differences in structure were also important: the AFL unions were craft-oriented, and though some of them had discarded their craft boundaries and were transformed into quasi-industrial organizations to compete with the CIO, the craft tradition remained strong. Their stock in trade was *jurisdiction*, spelled out in their charters and constitutions and regarded as property rights. The new CIO unions were industrial from the start, with wide jurisdictions embracing all the employees of a particular industry, skilled and unskilled alike. Reconciling these rival claims proved to be one of the most difficult problems facing the new Federation.

ETHICAL PRACTICES

The most immediate concern of the merged organization was corruption and undemocratic practices in some of its affiliated national unions. In January 1957, the United States Senate set up a Select Committee on Improper Activities in the Labor or Management Field, chaired by Senator John J. McClellan. Among its members was then Senator John F. Kennedy, while its chief counsel was Robert F. Kennedy. In a series of public hearings held during the next three years, a record of abuses committed by top officers of several unions emerged, casting a shadow over the entire labor movement.

The AFL had been aware of corruption in some of its affiliates, but believed that it was confined mainly to local situations and was left to national unions to clean up. The AFL had expelled the International Longshoremen's Association in 1953 after investigations revealed widespread racketeering on the New York and New Jersey waterfronts. One of the principal conditions insisted upon by the CIO was that power be vested in the Executive Council to deal with this problem. Article VIII, Section 7 of the AFL-CIO constitution conferred upon the Council authority to investigate "any situation in which there is reason to believe that any affiliate is dominated, controlled or substantially influenced in the conduct of its affairs by any corrupt influence" and to suspend any affiliate found permeated by such influence by a two-thirds vote, subject to final expulsion by the biennial convention. The constitution also provided for a committee on ethical practices to assist the Council in carrying out its mandate.

Even before the McClellan Committee had begun to hold hearings, the Executive Council received a report alleging corruption in three affiliated unions: the Laundry Workers, the Allied Industrial Workers, and the Distillery Workers. In August 1956, the Council concluded that the Distillery and Laundry unions were corrupt, and directed them to show cause why they should not be suspended. The ethical practices committee was directed to look further into the affairs of Allied Industrial. At a subsequent Council meeting in January 1957, all three were given ninety days to eliminate corruption and remove those responsible. Several months later the Laundry union was suspended, while no action was taken with respect to the others on condition that they agreed to be placed on probationary status for one year and to submit to an assessment of their operations by a special AFL-CIO representative. The Allied Industrial union accepted this condition and was soon restored to good standing. The Distillery Workers, after several years on probation, was also cleared. The Laundry Workers were expelled by the 1957 convention and steps were taken to replace it with a new union composed initially of breakaway locals.

In a move to counter adverse public opinion fueled by the revelations of the McClellan Committee, the 1957 AFL-CIO convention adopted a series of codes designed to provide a mechanism for self-policing. Had they been in effect earlier, there might have been no Senate Committee investigation. The first code, entitled Paper Locals, dealt with local unions that had fallen into the hands of corrupt individuals who used them for illicit purposes. According to the sponsors of the code, "These racketeers victimized workers, employers, and the public, and gave a black eye to the labor movement. Such charters enabled them to invade the jurisdictions of legitimate unions." Affiliates were enjoined to follow the principle of issuing local charters only upon application of a minimum number of workers in the trade or industry involved. They were directed "to insure the forthwith withdrawal of local union charters which have been issued and are now outstanding in violation of these policies."

This code was aimed at a practice the McClellan Committee found to prevail in a number of cities. For example, in the coin-operated machine industry of Chicago, criminals have used captive labor union locals to dominate various parts of the industry. They have had little trouble obtaining racket locals for their own use. As honest labor leaders have withdrawn charters from locals perverted to nontrade union objectives, an increasing number of racket locals have taken over the field.

These locals were characterized by high dues, small membership, financing by employers, agreements in which the employees had no voice, and officers with criminal records.[1]

The second ethical practice code dealt with health and welfare funds. Designed to safeguard one of the largest types of funds entrusted to unions, it forbade union officials who were receiving full-time salaries from securing fees of any kind from such funds, even when serving as trustees. Nor were they permitted to maintain any personal ties with insurance carriers, brokers, or consultants doing business with welfare plans. Complete records were required to be kept, audited regularly, and made available to the beneficiaries. Competitive bidding by potential carriers was mandated, and fund reserves were not to be invested in the business of any contributing employer.

Misuse of welfare funds for the personal gain of union officers was found by the McClellan Committee in several unions, where kickbacks were made to trustees responsible for placing money. An example:

The teamster leaders have entered into highly improper business relationships with the insurance companies which handle the millions of dollars of health, welfare and pension funds. They have approached banks which are the repositories of the accounts of union funds for special favors and loans at unusually low rates of interest.[2]

The third code dealt with racketeers, crooks, communists, and fascists. By 1957, the communist issue, which had troubled the CIO, had been settled by the expulsion from the CIO of a number of communist-dominated unions. This code was aimed primarily at dishonest officials at both the national and local level. Unions were told that it was not necessary to wait for convictions before removing such officials, but to make determinations "as a matter of common sense and with due regard to the rights of the labor unions and the individuals involved." Persons who were convicted of any crime involving moral turpitude were to be removed, and no one was to hold union office "who is commonly known to be a crook or racketeer preying on the labor movement and its good name for corrupt purposes, whether or not previously convicted for such nefarious activities."

Alex Rose, head of the Hatters Union, provided the 1957 AFL-CIO convention an example of the kind of official to whom this code would apply. He said that James Cross, president of the Bakery Workers, was

in the racket of unethical behavior, of extravagance, of conflict of interests, of corrupt influence, and I may say of terrorism within the organization itself. . . . It is this James

Cross who is in the eyes of public opinion, in the eyes of public opinion stands as a symbol of selfishness, of corruption and of betrayal of labor trust.[3]

The fourth code dealt with the investments and business interests of union officials. While they were at liberty to invest in publicly traded securities in firms or industries unrelated to the areas in which their unions operated, they could not have any interests in firms with which they bargained, or competing firms. The McClellan Committee found that officers of the Operating Engineers "entered into business arrangements with the very employers with whom they negotiate in what the committee feels are clear conflicts of interests."[4]

The fifth code related to the financial practices of unions. The Executive Council affirmed that unions are not profit-making institutions and that their funds should be invested in accordance with strict fiduciary standards. Officers were not to benefit personally from commercial transactions in which their unions were involved, nor to borrow from unions for their personal business affairs. But what of situations that have arisen in recent years in which unions have given assistance to firms, either in the form of monetary loans or wage and other concessions, in order to keep the firms afloat? This problem is considered below.

The sixth and final code involved union democratic processes. This code required that every union member have the right to full participation in union governance; to fair treatment in the application of union rules; and to criticize policies and personalities in the organization without undermining its existence. Regular conventions were to be held at not more than four-year intervals and were to be open to the public. National unions were to discipline locals in strict accord with the union constitution.

In addition to these codes, by a vote of 22 to 1 the Council resolved that a union official who invoked the Fifth Amendment to the U.S. Constitution to avoid testifying before appropriate legislative committees or other public bodies had no right to continue in office. The negative vote was cast by Dave Beck, president of the Teamsters and at the time a member of the Council. Walter Reuther stated that in his view, testifying and turning records over to a legislative committee would not impinge on union autonomy. Shortly after this action, Beck invoked the Fifth Amendment before the McClellan Committee. Meany recommended that he be suspended while the charges against him were being investigated by the AFL-CIO ethical practices committee, and this was agreed upon. The Council later determined that he was guilty of gross misuse of union funds, and it expelled him.

As the litany of Teamster malfeasance unfolded before the McClellan Committee, the AFL-CIO leadership was confronted with a difficult task. The Teamsters Union was the central target of the Committee, and what emerged was an incredible list of corrupt practices by Beck and other officials. Beck used union funds freely for his own personal expenses, even very trivial ones; he entered into profitable relationships with employers with whom the union was bargaining. He emerged as the most dishonest figure in the history of American labor. He was subsequently convicted of tax evasion and grand larceny, and served a term in prison.

Other top officers of the Teamsters were directed to appear before the ethical practices committee to answer the various allegations that had been made against them by the McClellan Committee. When they did not appear, the Council resolved to call upon the union to remove all corrupt officers and to agree to the appointment of a special committee to oversee its affairs, warning that failure to accede would bring the question of its expulsion before the next AFL-CIO convention. The Council observed: "We exceedingly regret the necessity for this action. We acutely recognize that it is no light matter to suspend from affiliation America's largest trade union. However, we are sworn to uphold the AFL-CIO Constitution."

The Teamsters presented this ultimatum to their own convention, and the answer was to elect James R. Hoffa to the presidency. Hoffa had also taken the Fifth Amendment before the McClellan Committee and had been linked to gangsters by witnesses. When the Teamsters' issue came before the AFL-CIO convention, John English, a Teamster delegate, argued that his union had protected the labor movement for many years and asked for delay of a year to clean itself up. He was supported by the presidents of the Upholsterers, the Sheet Metal Workers, the Typographers, and the Pattern Makers. The convention voted to expel by a 4 to 1 margin, with twenty-five national unions voting with the minority. Despite reluctance to see this large and powerful union go, any other course of action may have led to a split in the Federation, since action against corruption was a major condition of the merger.

This did not clear the decks, since several other unions had been castigated by the McClellan Committee. Among them was an old AFL union, the Bakery and Confectionery Workers, whose president, James Cross, was charged with using union funds for his personal expenses. The union was directed to restore to office its secretary-treasurer, who had been expelled for opposing Cross, and to convene a special convention to get rid of other corrupt officers. When it failed to comply, it was expelled and took with it 136,000 members. A new union, the American Bakery Workers, was chartered almost immediately and was joined by thirty-six breakaway locals. The two groups were merged in 1969 after the Bakery Workers had purged the offending officers.

Of the officers of the United Textile Workers Union (formerly AFL), the McClellan Committee had this to say:

As an unblushing exercise in avarice, the union careers of Anthony Valente and Lloyd Klenert can scarcely be matched. . . . While much larger sums of money have been misused for personal profit and pleasure by other officials interrogated by the committee, in relative terms the peculations of Valente and Klenert were far more spectacular. The UTWA's wealth is comparatively small; its annual income is less than $1 million. The funds misappropriated totaled $178,000, or about 18 percent of the union's entire intake in any one year.[5]

The UTW was placed on probation after Valente and Klenert were removed, although the union softened the blow by voting them long-term payments of $140,000. Probation was lifted in 1960.

Several other unions received bad notices from the McClellan Committee, including the Meat Cutters, the Hotel and Restaurant Employees, the Operating Engineers, and the Sheet Metal Workers. Apart from the Operating Engineers, however, these involved local situations with which the parent could deal. In the case of the latter, a key construction union, the Committee stated:

In the American labor movement, the International Union of Operating Engineers stands out as an ugly example of ruthless domination of working men and women through violence, intimidation and other dictatorial practices. . . . Democracy within this vital union is virtually nonexistent.[6]

William E. Maloney, the union president, misused hundreds of thousands of dollars, and when he resigned at the conclusion of the hearings the union conferred a $50,000 a year pension upon him. The union itself agreed to accept recommendations made by the ethical practices committee and to report to Meany periodically on their implementation.

Another remnant of the past was cleared up. The AFL had expelled the International Longshoremen's Association (ILA) and chartered a new one in its place. A million dollars were spent to bolster this organization but without success. The ILA applied for readmission in 1959, claiming that it had met the conditions laid down by the AFL. It was reinstated on the union's commitment to eliminate bad practices, including racial discrimination. The AFL was unable to overcome the loyalty of its membership to officers with dubious records.

The AFL-CIO had hoped that by cleaning its own house, remedial legislation could be avoided. But this was not to be. Meany hoped that in return for adopting the ethical practices code and disciplining offending unions, some of the provisions of the Taft-Hartley Act, notably those dealing with secondary boycotts, would be repealed, but there was little chance of that. A relatively mild Kennedy-Ives bill was passed by the Senate despite opposition of the Eisenhower administration, but it was killed in the House. The Executive Council said of that proposal: "Although the measure was not perfect, and imposed substantial regulation on the labor movement, we supported it in the public interest as, on balance, a much-needed reform measure."[7] A revised version of Kennedy-Ives was introduced in 1959 that authorized prehire agreements in the building industry and allowed economic strikers to vote in National Labor Relations Board (NLRB) elections, among other things. This also failed passage.

Finally, after a good deal of political infighting, Congress enacted the Labor-Management Reporting and Disclosure Act, popularly known as the Landrum-Griffin Act, in September 1959 (the Senate by a vote of 95 to 1 and the House by 352 to 52) after Eisenhower had urged its adoption in a radio address. This represented a bitter defeat for labor, which objected particularly to a so-called bill of rights that had been added to the original anticrime provisions under employer pressure. The next AFL-CIO convention denounced it as a measure

designed to destroy organized labor but we will not be destroyed. . . . We shall make unmistakably clear that the so-called reform bills are part of the carefully planned campaign of Big Business to seize absolute control of industrial life in the United States.[8]

Among labor's specific objections were the following:

1. Although detailed reporting requirements were imposed on unions, there were no similar requirements on employers with respect to their industrial relations activities.
2. Government control was injected deeply into the internal structure of unions.
3. Unions would be hamstrung by rigid restrictions on the handling of finances.
4. There was a blunderbuss approach in that detailed requirements were applied to all unions regardless of size and structure.
5. Union officers could be removed for reasons other than corruption, thus creating turmoil.
6. The supervisory functions allocated to the Department of Labor completely altered its historical functions and responsibilities.
7. The legislation ignored the efforts of the labor movement itself to get rid of corruption.
8. The secondary boycott provisions strengthened the prohibitions in the Taft-Hartley Act, particularly with respect to ''hot cargoes.''
9. Organizational and recognition picketing were banned under circumstances which led to the frustration of organizing campaigns.
10. The provisions for pre-hiring contracts in construction were foolish and ineffective.[9]

The new law had one adverse effect on the ability of the Federation to police its affiliates. If the officers of a union were called before the ethical practices committee to explain their activities, there would be a natural reluctance for them to confess to any sins since they might also be under investigation by a government agency. In a sense, any action taken by the committee would be duplicating procedures under Landrum-Griffin.

The AFL-CIO had devoted its resources and influence to defeat this legislation, and its enactment represented a major blow so early in its new life. Congressional action was fueled by the large volume of antiunion media publicity that accompanied the McClellan Committee hearings. Protestations that only a handful of national unions were involved were muffled by the lurid revelations of what had been going on in the Teamsters Union, and many felt that earlier action should have been taken to expel an organization that was widely reputed to be infiltrated by criminals. The CIO had to rid itself of communist influence in order to maintain intact its reputation as a democratic organization. Had the AFL acted a decade earlier, it might have averted the adverse publicity of the years 1956 to 1960 and not opened itself to the widespread criticism promoted by the foes of the labor movement.

JURISDICTION

The second difficult problem faced by the AFL-CIO in its early existence was sorting out the economic sectors in which affiliates were to operate. The merger agreement provided that "each affiliated union should have the same organizing jurisdiction in the merged federation as it had in its respective prior organization." Where there were conflicting jurisdictions, "affiliates of the merged federation will be encouraged to eliminate conflicts and duplications through the process of agreement, merger, or other means, by voluntary agreement with the appropriate officials of the merged federation." In fact, two years before the merger took effect, the parties had entered into a no-raiding agreement.

The AFL-CIO constitution contains detailed provisions for handling jurisdictional disputes. Briefly, it defines the bargaining relationships that must be honored by affiliates, and provides for a panel of mediators to handle rival claims to jurisdiction and of umpires in the event that mediation proves unsuccessful. Appeals from decisions of umpires may be lodged with the Executive Council, as well as complaints that such decisions have not been honored. Penalties for refusal to abide by Executive Council determinations are specified, including denial of all Federation services and facilities. However, this article of the constitution did not take effect until January 1, 1962. Prior to that date, disputes were handled under the earlier no-raiding agreement.

It was not long before jurisdictional conflict arose. In 1956, the Executive Council was called upon to settle disputes between the Carpenters and the Upholsterers and between the Railway Clerks and the Machinists. The Director of Organization reported that jurisdictional strife between two unions of textile workers was hindering a drive to organize the South, and he was authorized to conduct the campaign regardless of whether the two settled their differences. An interesting case was denial of the application of the National Agricultural Workers Union to organize small farms on the ground that the AFL-CIO was an organization of employees and not of independent entrepreneurs. This was in line with earlier denial of a request by the Office Employees Union to organize chiropractors.

Not unexpectedly, the industrial-craft union controversy that had been the major reason for the foundation of the CIO in 1935 soon emerged. Conflicting resolutions on jurisdiction by the Building Trades and Industrial Union Departments were referred by the 1957 convention to the Executive Council for resolution. The Council responded by setting up a joint committee of the two departments, which agreed to send special representatives into the field when disputes arose. By 1959, although many problems remained, procedures and formulae had been installed in many localities. An agreement was also reached

that new construction should be done by the building trades and current maintenance by industrial workers. Past practice was to govern in the gray area in
between. However, not all unions subscribed to the agreement.

There were a reported two hundred disputes a year between the building and
industrial unions. Walter Reuther was particularly vehement in denouncing
them:

I say that jurisdictional problems are wrong. They are anti-social, they are anti-labor,
and we need to find the answer to these problems on a live-and-let-live basis in which
the equity of every union, large or small, craft or industrial, is given its rightful place in
this united labor movement.[10]

A particularly egregious example of a craft-industrial dispute involved the
Sheet Metal Workers and the Steelworkers at a plant of the Carrier Corporation.
The latter union had won a representation election but the company refused to
recognize it, leading to a strike. The Sheet Metal Workers petitioned for a new
election and refused to withdraw when the Executive Council urged that it do
so, for which it was censured by the 1961 convention. Neither union came out
ahead in the end. This episode illustrates the adverse impact of jurisdictional
disputes on organization.

The industrial unions favored strengthening the disputes mechanism by requiring compulsory arbitration as the last step, but this was strongly opposed
by the crafts, with whom Meany sided. The traditional aversion of AFL unions
to final determination by outsiders was too strong to be overcome.

There were some mergers, the most effective way of settling jurisdictional
disputes, but most of the unions involved were relatively small and making
adjustments for leadership positions was not too difficult. Two unions of insurance workers with a combined membership of 22,000 were merged in 1959; a
thousand Engravers joined the Machinists; a thousand Wallpaper Craftsmen
merged with the Pulp and Paper Workers; and a thousand Wire Weavers joined
the Paper Makers. There was one merger between larger unions even this early
when 60,000 members of the Brotherhood of Paper Makers amalgamated with
40,000 United Paper Workers. As the years went by, mergers became more
frequent, spurred by membership decline and the rising financial cost of running
a union.

It did not take the now independent Teamsters long to transgress areas claimed
by AFL-CIO affiliates. The Teamsters were offering money and organizing assistance to unions willing to enter into alliance with them, a tempting offer for
struggling organizations. These efforts led Meany to call Hoffa Labor's Enemy
No. 1, ahead of the National Association of Manufacturers and the Chamber of
Commerce. The entire matter was discussed at a 1961 meeting of the Executive
Council. A convention of the Transport Workers Union had voted to invite the
Teamsters back. Woodruff Randolph of the Typographical Union, which had
long been an ardent proponent of the rights of individual unions, argued that

since Hoffa had never been convicted of a crime, he should be invited back if he were willing to abide by the ethical practices codes. William McFetridge of the Hotel Workers, a union for which Teamster support was often crucial, suggested that unless all AFL-CIO affiliates had cleaned up all their locals, the Teamsters should not be excluded. The Council rejected these appeals, with Randolph and Joe Curran of the Maritime Union voting against this decision.

There was some hope that the AFL-CIO might launch a new union to pick up dissident Teamster locals. A. J. Hayes of the Machinists complained that his union had been obliged to cancel a no-raiding agreement with the Teamsters and thought it might be useful to provide a haven for drivers who wanted to get out from under Hoffa. Meany was sympathetic and he pointed out that the Teamsters had amended their constitution to give them universal jurisdiction, which they exercised by raiding many AFL-CIO unions. It was finally agreed to accept dissident locals as direct affiliates of the AFL-CIO, a status accorded to groups insufficiently large to form a national body. In the event, the AFL-CIO took few such actions and never chartered a national union of drivers. To have done so would have meant all-out warfare with a powerful and firmly entrenched organization.

INDUSTRIAL RELATIONS

The years 1955 to 1960 were not unfavorable for labor economically. Average hourly earnings rose by 22.2 percent compared with a consumer price increase of 10.6 percent. However, the average unemployment rate was 6.1 percent. AFL-CIO membership increased by 600,000 from 1955 to 1957, then began to fall, and by 1961 was less than it had been at the time of the merger. The density ratio fell by 9 percent over this period.

Recession in 1958 did not foreclose wage gains. In addition, the supplemental unemployment benefit plans negotiated in the automobile industry in 1955 had their first extensive use in 1958, softening the impact of layoffs. Two-week vacations with pay after five years of service were becoming the norm. The duration of agreements was tending to be stretched to two or even three years, with annual wage reopenings. Automatic cost of living adjustments became common.

The onset of membership decline led to increased emphasis on organization. The AFL-CIO's Director of Organization pointed out in 1961 that 1.5 million workers had been organized since the merger, but an equal number had left. He called NLRB delays the most serious obstacle, with employer letters to their employees emphasizing union racketeering close behind. Other difficulties cited were pro-business attitudes of the Eisenhower administration, state right-to-work laws, and the growth of white-collar employment. Joseph Beirne of the Communications Workers observed that technicians were particularly difficult to organize: "They consider themselves to a great extent above the mass worker movement. They in effect due to their considered superior education look down their noses at you and me. . . . They are not in substance good material today for trade union membership.''[11]

Of the nine million people working in the public sector in 1961, only 15 percent were unionized, with the same percentage for retail and wholesale trade. The fact that a number of unions were trying to organize the same establishments did not help. The Teamsters were an ever-present danger. The American Federation of Teachers, seeking a subsidy for organizing in New York, quoted a pamphlet by the rival independent National Education Association (NEA) that read: ''A chunk of every person's dues is chopped off willy-nilly to the AFL-CIO headquarters to bankroll actions that teachers may have no interest in, or even actively oppose.'' They succeeded in having the 1957 convention brand the NEA a company union.

These years were marked by a number of sizable strikes. The O'Sullivan Company, the nation's largest producer of rubber heels, was closed down by 15,000 employees and put on the AFL-CIO boycott list. The Brewery Workers mounted a strike against Coors Brewery, which was to have troubled industrial relations for years. The Retail Clerks struck Montgomery-Ward after five months of negotiations. A quarter of a million General Motors workers went out on October 4, 1958, when GM refused to accept the terms of an agreement reached with Ford and Chrysler. Caterpillar Tractor was shut down by 20,000 workers, and Pittsburgh Plate Glass and Libby-Owens by 27,000 workers.

Among the other leading firms that experienced work stoppages were all the major airlines, Allis-Chalmers, U.S. Rubber, Firestone, and the entire steel industry. A controversy that had interesting implications for the future arose when the Screen Actors Guild called a strike against movie producers to obtain a share of the royalties when pictures were sold to the television industry. When Universal International conceded to the Guild on this issue, the Guild president, Ronald Reagan, called on the other producers to show the same sense of responsibility and sign up.

An employer campaign to induce individual states to adopt right-to-work laws and thus outlaw union shop agreements was beginning to make headway. A committee headed by Eleanor Roosevelt and former Senator Herbert Lehman to fight these laws was formed, but by 1960 nineteen states had enacted such legislation. The unions began a campaign to organize farm workers and the Executive Council chartered the Agricultural Workers Organizing Committee and appropriated $100,000 to support it.

An index of the overall relationship between the AFL-CIO and the Eisenhower administration was a union-sponsored dinner for James P. Mitchell, the Secretary of Labor. President Eisenhower dropped in to say a few words. George Meany, who was unavoidably absent, telegraphed that ''we are publicly reiterating our belief that Jim Mitchell is not only an able and conscientious public servant, but he is also a friend of labor and a fine man.''[12] These seem like distant times.

A resolution introduced at the 1959 convention proposed an amendment to the AFL-CIO constitution that would have required all affiliates to adhere to AFL-CIO central bodies, state and local. State federations in particular complained that they were not receiving sufficient support from unions in their areas. Meany opposed a mandatory requirement on the ground that it would change the voluntary nature of the Federation, and the resolution was defeated. However, this matter would come up repeatedly later.

In sum, the first five years after the merger were difficult ones for the new Federation, but it weathered them rather well. There were many strikes, mostly successful. The corruption issue was beginning to fade away. Progress had been made in fitting the two rival federations together, despite their previous antagonism. Meany was justified in reporting to the 1959 convention that

the merger is working out well. There have been, of course, occasional differences of opinion over methods and jurisdiction, but these can be expected within any family and they are gradually being ironed out. On all major questions of policy, however, our united federation has acted with decisive unanimity. No longer in America can our enemies turn divided factions of labor against each other. We have cemented a united front.[13]

NOTES

1. U.S. Senate, "Final Report of the Select Committee on Improper Activities in the Labor or Management Field," Part 4, March 31, 1960, pp. 857–858.
2. U.S. Senate, "Interim Report of the Select Committee on Improper Activities in the Labor or Management Field," No. 1417, 1958, p. 445.
3. AFL-CIO, *Proceedings of the Second Constitutional Convention*, 1957, p. 227.
4. U.S. Senate, "Interim Report of the Select Committee," p. 438.
5. Ibid., p. 159.
6. Ibid., p. 437.
7. *AFL-CIO News*, August 30, 1958.
8. AFL-CIO, *Proceedings of the Third Constitutional Convention*, 1959, p. 613.
9. *AFL-CIO News*, February 14, 1959; *American Federationist* (August 1960), p. 2.
10. *AFL-CIO News*, November 9, 1957.
11. AFL-CIO, *Proceedings of the Second Constitutional Convention*, 1957, p. 319.
12. *AFL-CIO News*, July 7, 1960.
13. AFL-CIO, *Report of the Executive Council to the Third Constitutional Convention*, 1959, p. 2.

CHAPTER 3

The Kennedy-Johnson Years

The 1960 election victory of John F. Kennedy, who had received strong AFL-CIO support, presaged renewed growth and influence for the labor movement. Arthur Goldberg, the architect of the merger, was appointed Secretary of Labor. Soon after his inauguration Kennedy named a tripartite labor-management policy committee with seven representatives of each of the parties and chaired by Goldberg to provide advice on wage and price policy. Included among the management members were heads of some of the largest companies in the country.

CIVIL RIGHTS AND AFFIRMATIVE ACTION

The merger agreement had provided that the new Federation

shall constitutionally recognize the right of all workers, without regard to race, creed, color or national origin to share in the full benefits of trade union organization in the merged federation. The merged federation shall establish appropriate internal machinery to bring about, at the earliest date, the effective implementation of this principle of non-discrimination.

This commitment was set forth in Article II (4) of the AFL-CIO constitution.

The Brotherhood of Locomotive Firemen and Engineers applied for a charter in the summer of 1956. It was granted with a promise to remove a color bar from its constitution. Vice-President A. Philip Randolph dissented. A year later, the Brotherhood of Railway Trainmen, which also excluded blacks from membership, applied for admission. Randolph again spoke in opposition, and this time the matter was put aside for further discussion. Several months later the Trainmen were given a charter.

Randolph, president of the all-black Brotherhood of Sleeping Car Porters, was the leading protagonist of affirmative action for working people. His union had been chartered in 1935 after the jurisdictional claims of other unions had been settled. One of the techniques he used in agitating for human rights was to rise at AFL conventions and read out the names of unions that barred blacks. Officers of offending unions would bargain with him for omission from his list by showing that they were making progress in meeting his objectives. In the spring of 1941 he organized a march on Washington to protest black exclusion from the defense industry, resulting in an executive order by President Roosevelt stipulating that all defense contracts contain nondiscrimination clauses and setting up a Committee on Fair Employment Practices to police the requirement.

The 1957 AFL-CIO convention resolved that the Federation support the national fair employment practices act. Randolph praised the activities of the AFL-CIO civil rights committee, but pointed out that there were still some affiliates with constitutional color bars and others that practiced discrimination. In a debate at the 1959 AFL-CIO convention Randolph objected to the readmission of the Longshoremen's union on the ground that it practiced discrimination. Meany replied with some asperity: "I never knew of discrimination in the ILA [International Longshoremen's Association]. It has Negro officials, Negro members, as long as I have known them. Its first vice-president for many years was a Negro. . . . I would like Brother Randolph to stay a little closer to the trade union movement and pay a little less attention to outside organizations that render lip service rather than real service."[1] Admission of the ILA was approved.

Randolph returned to the attack at the convention with the assertion that the promises of the railway unions had not been fulfilled and urged that they be suspended. The convention resolutions committee proposed that the matter be turned over to the Executive Council for action, and again Randolph objected. He observed that no Negro had ever been employed as a railroad engineer in the South and that Negro firemen were currently being displaced. George Meany argued for more time to work with the offending unions, and the motion to delay carried.

The debate resumed over a resolution condemning segregated locals. Harry Bates, the venerable president of the Bricklayers Union, asserted that some of his black locals preferred to remain that way. In fact, this was true of other unions, particularly in the building trades. Because they were not accepted in white locals, blacks organized segregated locals that managed to carve out jurisdictional niches they were reluctant to abandon. When Randolph denounced this practice, Meany declared, "I am for the democratic rights of the Negro members. Who appointed you the guardian of the Negro members in America. You talk about tolerance." Whereupon Randolph replied, "I don't believe that a group of Negro members of a union have a right to maintain a Jim Crow local if we believe in an accepted trade union policy."[2] This exchange marked a low point in the long relationship of the two men.

The next flare-up came at a meeting of the Executive Council in February,

1961. Randolph complained that the AFL-CIO civil rights committee had been doing a poor job recently, and he urged that efforts be made to bring the Federation and the Negro community closer together. He proposed that all unions set up civil rights departments, that more Negroes be chosen as convention delegates, and that separate seniority rosters for blacks and whites be forbidden. Meany defended the AFL-CIO record, and was backed by the Council. However, the Council did adopt a statement endorsing fair employment legislation, a campaign against segregated locals, and a recommendation that all national unions establish civil rights committees.

At an October meeting of the Council later in the year Randolph once more expressed his dissatisfaction with the tempo of Federation action. He termed it "distressing, innocuous, sterile and barren of any creative, broad changing ideas that can give strength and force to the Civil Rights movement in the AFL-CIO for the elimination of racial bias." The response was that expulsion of unions was not an effective solution, for once they were outside the Federation they would simply continue their previous conduct. Randolph was accused of not lifting a finger against the deliberate defamation of organized labor. A punitive program, it maintained, was inconsistent with voluntarism. He had derogated the AFL-CIO drive against discrimination and had to share responsibility for the gap between organized labor and the Negro community. His proposals that unions be urged to elect Negro delegates to AFL-CIO conventions was unacceptable, because it would entail a choice based on color.

Part of the reason for this blast was the formation of the Negro American Labor Council, with Randolph at its head. The Council had not cooperated with the AFL-CIO on civil rights, and had publicly criticized it. The fear was that this body would create a labor movement similar to the AFL-CIO, but such a situation never materialized.

The AFL-CIO was moving ahead on discrimination, if too slowly for Randolph. Its 1961 convention called for the strengthening of union compliance with civil rights requirements, particularly with respect to segregated locals. It came down squarely in favor of a law on fair employment practices. Randolph wanted a code of fair union racial practices similar to those on ethics. Walter Reuther, whose union had been in the forefront of the civil rights movement, supported Randolph. But the idea was defeated on Meany's insistence that the impetus should come at the local level.

The Executive Council issued a directive barring AFL-CIO central bodies from holding conventions where provision of lodging and food was discriminatory. A survey conducted in 1963 indicated that there were 172 segregated locals out of 55,000 in all AFL-CIO unions. For their part, several national unions complained that the National Association for the Advancement of Colored People (NAACP) was sponsoring decertification petitions with the NLRB where it regarded contracting locals to be discriminatory.

In August 1963, Randolph led a march on Washington at which Martin Luther King made his famous speech. Reuther proposed that the march be endorsed by the AFL-CIO and that all affiliates be asked to participate. The Executive Council questioned whether the labor movement should be identified with a demonstration over which it had no control. The outcome was a statement supporting the rights of marchers and the freedom of affiliates to participate-but no endorsement.

However, by the end of 1963, when the Civil Rights bill was being debated in Congress, the AFL-CIO had come out in full support of the fight for racial equality. In his message to the 1963 convention, Meany declared:

During the last two years a revolution has swept across the United States, north and south, a peaceful revolution, though sometimes met with violent opposition, through which Negro Americans have sought fulfillment of the rights that have been theirs by law for a hundred years. The AFL-CIO wholeheartedly supports that aim, and is proud that the labor movement has fought for it for more than a generation.[3]

The civil rights legislation submitted to Congress by the Kennedy administration did not contain a section on equal employment rights. Under pressure from the AFL-CIO such a section was added, and after months of delay, President Johnson signed it into law on July 4, 1964. Randolph told the Executive Council in a meeting a few months later that the AFL-CIO had done a tremendous job in helping pass the Civil Rights Act. There was no longer any talk of separatism; Negroes must now stand with the AFL-CIO and join its unions.

A. Philip Randolph died in May 1979, at the age of 90. An institute has been established in his name to carry on his work, to which the AFL-CIO has made regular annual contributions. A lifelike bust of Randolph, in a characteristic pose, stands in the main concourse of Union Station in Washington, a fitting tribute to a man who was the conscience of the American labor movement for fifty years, and more than anyone else helped win equal employment rights for black Americans.

ORGANIZING

The Democratic administration that gained office in 1961 offered the unions an opportunity to reverse the decline that had characterized the Eisenhower years. There was more sympathy in Washington for the union cause and less pro-employer bias. In fact, although AFL-CIO density fell from 1961 to 1969, it would have remained unchanged had it not been for the resignation of the Automobile Workers in 1968.

Jack Livingston, the AFL-CIO Director of Organization, reported in 1960 that almost a million white-collar workers were employed by the Federal government; more than a million by state governments, a third of them in schools; three and a half million by local governments; 120,000 by the Bell Telephone system; five million by retail shops; and 700,000 by the insurance industry. Not many out of this potentially rich pool had been brought into unions. On the other hand, 85 percent of blue-collar workers were already organized in situations where organization was feasible.

The AFL-CIO leadership realized that the changing character of the labor force had to be taken into account in new efforts to expand membership. It was decided that a permanent standing committee on organization was to be set up and that the staff of the Department of Organization should be increased. Meany pointed to the lack of solidarity among unions as a obstacle to organization. Some were inactive in their claimed jurisdictional areas and only stepped in when other unions initiated organizing drives there, to the detriment of all.

A resolution adopted at the 1961 convention listed employer resistance, hostile mass media, and union rivalry as the main obstacles to unionism. Reuther urged the institution of coordinated membership drives with special attention to white-collar and service employees. He offered a million dollars on behalf of his union toward a special organizing fund and denounced paper jurisdictional claims.

The Executive Council instructed the Department of Organization to encourage the development of cooperative drives among unions and to work out specific targets in advance to avoid the dissipation of resources. Where the Department was providing assistance to an affiliate, other affiliates were to be denied the right to "block such organizational assistance by the exercise of a paper claim to jurisdiction or for reasons of a completely negative obstructionist attitude."

A pilot coordinated campaign was inaugurated in Los Angeles, in which specific enterprises were assigned to individual unions. There were 5,000 union officers in the area who were urged to work together rather than compete. Four major divisions were established: manufacturing, government, hotels and restaurants, and residential construction. Some 500 enterprises were targeted and fifty unions were involved. It was the most ambitious organizing effort since the great drives of the 1930s.

The initial results were favorable. Of more than 500 representation elections held, only nine involved more than one AFL-CIO union. Sixty thousand workers became members in two years. Interunion cooperation in finding new jobs for victimized workers, the exchange of organizers among unions, and mass demonstrations were effective devices that were used. One of the most celebrated open-shop symbols on the West Coast, the Harvey Aluminum Company, was organized.

A similar campaign was initiated in the Washingon-Baltimore area, concentrating on public employees. Maine, Indiana, and Iowa were also targeted, as well as Atlanta, Georgia, with generally favorable initial results. National and local meetings with NLRB officials were held to discuss Board procedures, events that were difficult to arrange before 1961. One result was an increase in the percentage of union election victories.

With these geographically-oriented campaigns under way, emphasis shifted to specific industries and corporations, the latter where a single company dominated an industry. Graphic arts and shipyards were examples of the former, General Electric of the latter. Increased attention was paid to professional and clerical employees. In general, the Kennedy-Johnson years were marked by a high level of organizing activity by the AFL-CIO and its constituent unions. They were not sitting back and letting economic events, particularly changes in the structure of the labor force, take their toll. The merger finally appeared to be paying off. Yet a resolution introduced in the 1969 convention by the Industrial Union Department struck a cautionary note:

There is reason to believe that workers will organize if they are convinced that they have something to gain. What they have to gain is not often as clear as it was to workers 30 years ago, especially when employer paternalism seems to provide comparable material benefits to those in union shops. The greatest values of organization go far beyond wage rates, but they are harder to make clear.[4]

JURISDICTION

It was during the 1960s that the pattern of dealing with jurisdictional disputes became fixed. Article XX (originally XXI) of the AFL-CIO constitution became effective on January 1, 1962. Unlike the no-raiding agreement, which bound only those unions that had signed it (105 of the 140 unions in the separate AFL and CIO), the new provisions were binding on all. The first step in the disputes process was mediation, followed by submission to an impartial umpire. His decision could be appealed to a subcommittee of the Executive Council, then to the Council as a whole. If an affiliate refused to abide by the decision, the Federation could publicize the fact and deny the offender any assistance. Other affiliates could be enjoined from rendering it any help, such as financial aid during a strike. By the end of 1970, some 1,075 complaints had been filed, averaging 119 a year, not a small number. Of these, 665 were settled at the mediation stage and 462 were submitted to an umpire. The Executive Council received 154 appeals, and filed 49 noncompliance charges, although only a handful of unions were eventually sanctioned.

David T. Cole, the umpire during this period, outlined some of the difficulties that arose in interpreting Article XX. For example, if a union that had an established bargaining relationship with an enterprise was decertified by the NLRB, could another union step in and seek to organize the employees involved? He held that it could not, thus affording the original union an opportunity to win over the employees once more. This was partly to prevent shopping by local officials who might be tempted to accept rival union offers and change their allegiances. Another example: Federal employees could gain informal, formal, or exclusive recognition, pursuant to a Kennedy executive order. The Executive Council ruled that a union might seek exclusive recognition notwithstanding lesser forms of recognition enjoyed by another union.

Many other problems arose, but the internal disputes procedure was off to a good start. Cole wrote:

Proceedings under the Internal Disputes Plan are being approached generally in a less tense and hostile manner than in the first years of the No-Raiding agreement. There is respect for those who carry out these necessary functions, and the deliberations of the Executive Council or its subcommittee, whether in appeals cases or when they are considering matters of a clarifying or policy nature, are taken very seriously.[5]

INTERNAL AFFAIRS

There were several matters during the early 1960s involving administration and structure that required action by the Council. One of them, reflecting lingering distrust between the two merger parties, involved election of a new member to the Council itself. At a meeting in October 1963, Reuther maintained that it had been understood that the ratio of seventeen to ten AFL and CIO members that prevailed at the time of the merger should continue. If this agreement were no longer in effect, the CIO members would refrain from voting. Meany's position was that it was never envisioned that vacancies would be filled by caucuses of each of the parties to the merger. He asserted that there was no agreement that the CIO members, by themselves, could fill a vacancy. In a vote to replace a retiring CIO member, five former CIO presidents abstained in protest. Article V of the AFL-CIO constitution provided that members were to be elected by the convention, but in fact Council nominees were always accepted.

To reflect the changing character of the Federation, a new trade group was established—the Food and Beverages Department. There had been six departments at the time of the merger, five inherited from the AFL and one from the Industrial Union Department created to accommodate the CIO. Historically, the Building Trades Department was the most important. In addition, a new staff echelon, the Department of Urban Affairs, was set up to deal with labor's interests in training, poverty, housing, and education. Further, a labor studies center was created to provide training for union officials.

The Federation manifested its interest in agricultural workers by financing an organizing campaign in 1959 and financing it to the tune of $427,000 for a two-year period. Eventually, the United Farm Workers Organizing Committee was chartered under the leadership of the charismatic Cesar Chavez. A year-long strike against California grape growers yielded contracts with some of the large growers, including DiGiorgio and Schenley. But these were only first steps in what turned out to be a long and arduous campaign. Members of the United Farm Workers union and their families fanned out all over the country in caravans financed by the Federation. There was a serious setback when DiGiorgio sold off its largest producing operations and ended its contract with the union.

Conservative groups, including the John Birch Society and the Farm Bureau Federation, joined the fray on the side of the employers. One of the union's chief difficulties was the ease with which Mexican workers could be imported, particularly because many held so-called green cards, enabling them to work in the United States despite the fact that they lived in Mexico most of the year. It was not until 1970 that the Farm Workers signed up the major grape growers and called off a national boycott that had been instituted.

The Federation had a brush with professionals when the independent Association of Scientists and Professional Engineers applied for a charter. Representing 1,500 employees of the Radio Corporation of America (RCA), it claimed that there were twenty similar groups representing 35,000 employees of industrial corporations waiting to be organized. A small union of technicians that had been in existence since 1918 objected to issuance of a charter to the RCA unit. The Council decided to hold the matter in abeyance but to maintain friendly relations with a new independent Council of Engineers and Scientists. This was a good example of an old union sitting on its jurisdictional rights without much activity.

An event that took place in 1963 was to be the source of later conflict. The Canadian Labor Congress (CLC) had been formed in the mid-1950s by the merger of two federations and became the dominant body of the Canadian labor movement. Many American unions had local unions in Canada, some of which affiliated with the CLC, leading to jurisdictional controversy. An AFL-CIO-CLC liaison committee agreed that the Canadian locals would be exempt from the American internal disputes mechanism, and the CLC promised to set up a similar plan. However, the CLC began chartering groups of workers which American unions were trying to organize, creating some bad feeling between the two federations.

THE ECONOMY

The economic conditions prevailing for most of the 1960s were favorable from a trade union standpoint. Prices were just beginning their upward course and wages were rising more rapidly, so that real earnings increased by an average of 2 percent a year. The average rate of unemployment from 1961 to 1968 was 4.9 percent.

To pay for the Great Society programs initiated by the Johnson administration, as well as the Vietnam war, the Executive Council favored increased taxes on corporate profits and greater progression in the income tax. It declared that if the President determined that a national emergency existed, the AFL-CIO would support wage restraints provided that similar measures were applied to all other categories—prices, profits, dividends, executive compensation. But it rejected wage restraints alone, such as the 3.2 percent guidelines recommended by the Council of Economic Advisers.

Toward the end of the decade unions were meeting greater employer opposition in collective bargaining, but they were nevertheless able to achieve favorable settlements. There were strikes against some major companies, including the *New York Times,* all the major airlines, and the big four copper companies. Payment for the rising commitment for men and materials to Vietnam was financed largely by government borrowing, creating serious problems for the following decades.

The Kennedy-Johnson years were the best ones for American labor since the New Deal; they were not matched in the years that followed. The AFL-CIO was consulted at the highest government levels, and many of the programs it supported were adopted. Among them were massive public works, public housing, hospital construction, Medicare, expansion of training, and improvements in the welfare system. Organized labor's influence on American life was at an all-time high. Kennedy told a convention of the Machinists Union in 1963: "I cannot think of a force over the last 30 years that has contributed more, not only to its own membership. . . . not only to the membership of the trade union movement, but for the well-being of our country." Not long after his inauguration President Johnson held a White House reception for 300 union leaders and asked their support for his war on poverty. Some palatial union headquarter buildings were appearing in Washington. The future seemed bright.

NOTES

1. AFL-CIO, *Proceedings of the Third Constitutional Convention,* 1959, p. 419.

2. Ibid., p. 630.

3. AFL-CIO, *Report of the Executive Council to the Fifth Constitutional Convention,* 1963, p. 1.

4. AFL-CIO, *Report of the Executive Council to the Eighth Constitutional Convention,* 1969, p. 270.

5. David T. Cole, "The Internal Disputes Plan a Working Reality," *American Federationist* (June 1969), p. 21.

CHAPTER 4

The Automobile Workers Disaffiliate

The year 1968 marked the end of an era in more than one respect. Constant friction between George Meany and Walter Reuther led to a break in the relationship between the United Automobile Workers Union (UAW) and the AFL-CIO. This rupture was slow in coming, but when it finally came, it did not happen quietly.

Given the personal histories of the two leaders and the different characteristics of the organizations they helped shape, the event seemed almost inevitable. George Meany had served an apprenticeship as a plumber in New York, then became a journeyman, a business agent for his local union, and, eventually, president of the New York State Federation of Labor. He became secretary-treasurer of the AFL in 1939, an unusual promotion for a man who did not head a national union. When William Green died in 1952, Meany succeeded him. Meany's close association with the building trades meant that he was brought up in the traditions of craft unionism and the core principle of jurisdiction. Voluntarism was also a key concept in the AFL; no union could be forced to accept the dictates of the AFL on jurisdiction or any other matter. Every affiliated union was sovereign.

Walter Reuther had a completely different background. In his youth a socialist, a working visit to the Soviet Union in the chaotic days of its first Five-Year Plan converted him to a strong anticommunist. Employed as a tool- and die-maker, he played a major role in the organization of the UAW. Although no longer a socialist, he became the spokesman for what started as a socialist faction in the union's bitter internecine fight. He became UAW president in 1946 and succeeded Philip Murray to the CIO leadership.

Reuther was a proponent of industrial unionism throughout his union career. Early efforts by the AFL to organize the auto workers by craft convinced most of the union activists that this was not feasible. He became a member of the UAW executive board at the age of 28 and served as an official of this liberal union for the rest of his life.

Reuther was a strong opponent of the communist faction in the UAW, which he eventually crushed. But his dislike of the Soviet Union and its disciples was overshadowed by Meany's fierce hatred of communism and all its works. Meany is said to have remarked on the occasion of President Richard Nixon's visit to China, "I used to be the number two anticommunist in the United States. Now I am number one."

Meany looked to Jay Lovestone for advice on foreign policy, which became another source of friction. Lovestone had been general-secretary of the American Communist Party from 1926 to 1929, when he was expelled for backing Nikolai Bukharin against Stalin in the struggle for power in the Soviet Union. After a short spell as the head of a new left-wing party that he organized, he became a rabid anticommunist and was employed as political adviser to the Ladies' Garment Workers Union, whose president, David Dubinsky, introduced him to Meany. Along the way, Lovestone and several of his followers became involved in an attempt to set up an AFL-sponsored automobile union in competition with the UAW, which earned him the latter's enmity. Lovestone eventually became the director of the AFL-CIO international affairs department in 1964. This paved the way for some bitter disagreements with Victor Reuther, Walter's brother, who directed international affairs for the UAW.

Some of the policy differences between Meany and Reuther have already been noted. Reuther had joined Randolph in criticizing the pace of desegregation by AFL-CIO affiliates. They were at odds on the manner in which Executive Council appointments were to be made. Reuther favored compulsory arbitration of jurisdictional disputes; Meany believed in voluntarism. Reuther was the only top white labor leader in the 1963 march on Washington.

The final straw was an incident at an International Labour Organization (ILO) meeting in Geneva. Rudy Faupl, the AFL-CIO delegate to an ILO conference, and his fellow delegates walked out in protest against the election of the Polish government delegate as conference president, the first time a communist was elected to that post. He called Meany before leaving, who replied:

You are the delegate, you are in a position to weigh the situation. If I were in your position I would do the same thing, but don't do anything that could commit the AFL-CIO to withdrawing from the Organization—which is a decision that neither you nor I can make but only the Executive Council.[1]

Upon being apprised of what had happened, Reuther addressed a letter to Meany, a copy of which was delivered to the *Washington Post* on the same day. In it he protested Faupl's action on the ground that the Executive Council had not had the opportunity to consider the decision before it was taken. He stated,

"The action of the delegates in walking out of the ILO Conference was unwise, undemocratic, contrary to established AFL-CIO policy, and unauthorized by any AFL-CIO body with authority to change that policy." Reuther demanded that Faupl and the other labor delegates be directed to resume their seats and continue to participate in the work of the conference.[2] Meany responded by calling a special meeting of the Council to discuss the matter.

Meany asserted at this meeting that the AFL-CIO convention, not he, made the Federation's foreign policy. He strongly denied an accusation Victor Reuther had made in an interview with the *Washington Post* that the American Institute for Free Labor Development (AIFLD), an AFL-CIO body supervised by Lovestone, had been receiving funds from the Central Intelligence Agency (CIA), but acknowledged that it had been getting money from AID, the government's development agency. Meany also said that he had discussed the Faupl withdrawal with President Lyndon Johnson, who had sent him to Dean Rusk, the Secretary of State. By this time the ILO conference was over, but Rusk urged that Faupl retain his seat on the ILO Governing Body, the ILO's executive committee.

Walter Reuther pointed out that the union delegates of all other countries had remained at the conference, and that Faupl's action represented a major policy change. It was his view that the AFL-CIO could not take on the communists alone, and that the best way to fight them was from within the ILO. To make things more tense, the UAW issued a press release while the Council meeting was in progress in which Reuther alleged that an ILO boycott had been under consideration at AFL-CIO headquarters a week before the walkout took place, which would have allowed ample time for discussion by the Council, an allegation that Meany branded a complete and total falsehood.

In the ensuing discussion, P. L. Siemiller, president of the Machinists, observed that the UAW was morally wrong in handling the matter through the press, while Dubinsky termed the entire episode painful. Jack Potofsky, a former CIO colleague of Reuther, called Faupl's action a mistake and supported the Reuther position though conceding that going public had been an error. The meeting ended with a motion in support of Meany and Faupl to the effect that withdrawal was the best way to protest the election of a totalitarian government representative to the ILO position. The vote was 18-6 in favor, with five members absent. In another Council meeting two months later, Reuther acknowledged that his brother had made a mistake in his reference to the CIA. After some discussion, a motion was adopted commending the AIFLD for its work, with Reuther and Joe Curran of the Maritime Workers voting no.

Reuther had asked for a special meeting of the Council to discuss foreign policy, and at his request it was held after the 1966 congressional elections. Reuther was not present, giving as an excuse the necessity of attending a special meeting of the UAW executive board. The Council meeting went ahead, nonetheless, and ended with the following unanimous statement:

We believe all our policies in this field should be continually re-evaluated on the basis of any new developments. This we have done for the past 11 years and this we will continue to do. Our judgment in all cases will continue to rest upon our unalterable devotion to freedom for all men in all places at all times.[3]

This only served to exacerbate the controversy. In a speech delivered a week later, Reuther told of his differences with Meany on foreign policy: He supported the test ban agreement with the USSR, Meany did not; he was for a more conciliatory policy than Meany on Vietnam. He stated:

But that is only a small part of the basic disagreement with this gentleman. Fundamentally, I disagreed because I believe that the American labor movement under his leadership is failing in the broad social responsibilities it has to the total community of America.[4]

He later said at a press conference that he stayed away from the November Council meeting that he had requested because his time was better spent elsewhere.

On December 28, 1966, Reuther sent an ''administrative letter'' to all UAW locals explaining his actions. Foreign policy gave way to a sweeping indictment of the AFL-CIO leadership, which was accused of complacency and adherence to the status quo and lack of social vision and the dynamic thrust that should characterize a modern labor movement. He cited disagreement on organizing the unorganized, including farm workers and the working poor; national wage and economic policy; labor disputes in the public sector; improvement of education, pension, and health benefits; the war on poverty; civil rights; the use of science and technology in rebuilding cities and rural areas; conservation of natural resources and prevention of air and water pollution; and relations with liberal intellectuals, academia, young people, and free world labor. Little was omitted.

The next move was a foregone conclusion. Reuther and the other three top officers of the UAW resigned from their AFL-CIO positions. This was followed by another ''administrative letter'' charging that the Council was ignoring convention decisions, violating the AFL-CIO constitution, and remaining impervious to new ideas and concepts. The Executive Council responded by asserting its complete adherence to constitutional requirements and proclaiming that all affiliates were free to present their positions at every opportunity afforded by the rules, with the stipulation that in order to have their programs and policies accepted they had to persuade the majority of their soundness.

A special UAW convention was called for April 20, 1967, at which Reuther explained what had happened and why. The Federation, he declared, had become stagnant with an acute case of hardening of the arteries, it had lost its drive, its vision had become blurred, its social idealism had become tarnished. The blame for failing to have vital legislation enacted was not attributable to the President of the United States nor Congress but to the labor movement itself. Why does labor have a bad image? He surmised, ''It comes together February of each year at the height of the tourist season, in the fanciest hotels on the gold-plated coast of Florida . . . one of the most notorious right-to-work states in the United States.''[5]

The UAW proposed an organizing crusade backed by an annual tax of one dollar a member levied on all unions. Jurisdictional claims had to be modified. It also proposed the creation of a central defense fund raised by an additional dollar tax. More effective bargaining structures had to be built, more attention paid to community problems. The guts of the problem, however, lay in internal reform of the Federation itself. Reuther favored expansion of the Executive Council to make it more representative. He believed that the small Executive Committee called for by the constitution had become moribund and in need of revival. He further felt that the General Board, meeting once a year, had become irrelevant and needed to be energized. The recommendations were drawn up in several detailed documents that would have transformed Federation structure and policy. Only five hands were raised at the UAW convention in opposition to a resolution conferring on the UAW Executive Committee the power to take any action it deemed necessary and appropriate with respect to the AFL-CIO.

This program was submitted in advance to the 1967 convention of the AFL-CIO in the form of a resolution. However, before the convention started the UAW informed Meany that it would not be represented at the convention and asked that the resolution be withdrawn. The excuse was that the UAW would be tied up in negotiations at the time of the convention. The next step was a UAW demand for a special AFL-CIO convention to consider its program. The UAW stated that if this were not granted, it would disaffiliate.

The Executive Council replied:

You can have a special convention on your charges and proposals as soon as it is humanly possible to hold one under these two conditions: 1. That you commit your organization without question to attend such a convention, if and when called. 2. That you further commit your organization to accept the democratically arrived at decision of such a convention.[6]

The UAW accepted the first condition but complained that the second violated the spirit and concept of a voluntary association and was both improper and unacceptable. Reuther told the next UAW convention that

they want us to have our hands tied behind us, sign a loyalty oath that will say that no matter what you do to us, we're going to stay put. . . . So we said to them, we are not going to stay under circumstances where our hands are tied. This is an autonomous International Union, and we are not going to go crawling to George Meany or anybody else at a special convention.[7]

What the UAW apparently planned to do was to put its per capita payment in escrow, allowing time to talk to its friends and see what positions they might adopt.

The Executive Council gave the UAW until May 15, 1968, to pay its per capita or stand suspended, which was in accord with the AFL-CIO constitution. This was done, and the UAW formally disaffiliated on July 1. The Executive Council submitted a long statement to the 1969 AFL-CIO convention refuting Reuther's charges point by point and labeling many of his statements falsehoods.

There was a good deal of speculation about the motives of Reuther and his associates in leaving the Federation. It is easy enough to read a personal vendetta between the two men and Reuther's disappintment at not somehow displacing Meany as head of the combined Federation as the main reasons. However, underlying personal ambitions and animosities were some fundamental differences regarding the nature and role of trade unions in American life.

The UAW was one of the most innovative and dynamic unions in the United States. It pioneered many of the fringe benefits that later spread—pensions and supplementary unemployment compensation among them. It took a leading role in the civil rights movement. While not avowedly socialist, it could have passed for a European social democratic union. In agreeing to the merger, the leaders of the UAW may have hoped that they might be able to revitalize a labor movement that they thought was still imbued with the philosophy of Samuel Gompers, one that did not act with sufficient promptness to root out corruption. As time went on it became clear that reform would be a slower process than they had anticipated. They learned that the term "business unionism" was not a pejorative one to their new associates who had grown and prospered under that concept. It was this perception that Reuther voiced when he said:

I was president of the national CIO and in that capacity. . . . I worked hard to bring about the merger of the AFL and the CIO. I shared the view that if we could build a united labor movement and get that labor movement on the march, we could do wonderful and exciting things in the United States. . . . It is nothing short of a great tragedy that the high hopes of the merger were not realized and this historic opportunity was wasted.[8]

How can this be reconciled with what followed? Within a few months after its departure from the AFL-CIO, the UAW entered into an agreement with the Teamsters and established the Alliance for Labor Action. Although Hoffa was gone, that union had not yet purged itself of corruption. The stated purpose of the Alliance was to organize the unorganized, strengthen collective bargaining, and deal with critical political, social, and economic problems. The two unions received equal representation in the administrative bodies. The Alliance was not to compete with the Federation, and a no-raiding agreement was offered to all AFL-CIO affiliates. Two major committees were set up, one on organizing and collective bargaining headed by Frank Fitzsimmons, president of the Teamsters, and the other on community and social action chaired by Reuther. The committees were staffed and ready for action by July 1969.

The UAW may have hoped that under its tutelage the power of the Teamsters could be harnessed in support of the liberal social policies embodied in the declaration of purpose and in the constitution of the Alliance. The Teamsters probably viewed this arrangement as a step toward respectability. It was certainly a marriage of convenience rather than of love.

If the founders of the Alliance expected to enlist other unions in their quest, they were disappointed. Only the Chemical Workers affiliated with it in return for a large loan. The president of this union defended the affiliation by pointing to the promised no-raid agreements, but George Meany declared, "We are told that this is not a rival federation. Well, I don't believe Walter. I know him and I just don't believe him." The Chemical Workers were expelled from the AFL-CIO, but a few years later they resigned from the Alliance and were readmitted.

This story does not have a happy ending. What might have happened to the Alliance, or to the labor movement, was foreclosed by Reuther's death in an airplane crash on May 9, 1970. The Alliance remained in existence until 1972, when it vanished. The UAW rejoined the AFL-CIO in 1981.

Walter Reuther was a controversial figure. The pact with the Teamsters tarnished his image. Nevertheless, whatever the motives behind his quarrel with the AFL-CIO, his place in the pantheon of the American labor movement is assured. Through his leadership of the UAW he opened new vistas not only for his own members, but for working people elsewhere. He set an example for the involvement of trade unions in seeking broad social change, particularly in the advancements of civil rights, and in the pursuit of democratic unionism. His tragic death at the height of his career deprived American labor of one of its most prescient and effective champions.

NOTES

1. AFL-CIO, *Report of the Executive Council to the Eighth Constitutional Convention,* 1969, p. 396.

2. Ibid., p. 398.

3. Ibid., p. 402.

4. Ibid., p. 403.

5. United Automobile Workers, *Proceedings of the Special Convention,* 1967, pp. 161 ff.

6. AFL-CIO, *Report of the Executive Council to the Eighth Constitutional Convention,* 1969, p. 424.

7. United Automobile Workers, *Proceedings of the Twenty-first Constitutional Convention,* 1968, p. 340.

8. United Automobile Workers, *Proceedings of the Special Convention,* 1967, p. 162.

CHAPTER 5

The Nixon-Ford Presidencies

The transition from a Democratic to a Republican administration went more smoothly for the labor movement than might have been expected. The new Secretary of Labor, George Shultz, was experienced in labor relations work. He appeared before the Executive Council shortly after Richard Nixon was inaugurated and read a letter from the President that said in part, "Together let us strive to strengthen the collective bargaining process and make it responsive to the needs of a changing economy, while preserving the freedom of private decision it guarantees." George Meany described the meeting as "constructive and cordial."

Although Shultz did not stay long at the Labor Department, relations between the AFL-CIO and the administration were cool but not hostile, at least in the early years. The Federation opposed two of Nixon's nominees to the Supreme Court, Clement F. Haynesworth and G. Harold Carswell, on the basis of their judicial records, the first time organized labor had come out against a nominee since 1930. One of the Haynesworth decisions that concerned the unions involved the Darlington Mills, a Southern textile company that had been carrying on a long struggle against efforts to organize it. A company owned in part by Haynesworth had significant contractual relations with Darlington which were not disclosed during litigation before his court. An examination of the record of the third nominee, Harry A. Blackmun, convinced the unions that he was not antilabor and they supported him. They were less successful in trying to block the appointment of Edward B. Miller, a management lawyer, to the National Labor Relations Board.

On Labor Day 1970, Nixon hosted a fete at the White House to which he invited a number of AFL-CIO officials. During the festivities Nixon proposed a toast to "the builders of America, those in American labor," and another to

"George Meany who stands for the best in free labor, for the best in America." Perhaps he was motivated by an Executive Council statement a few months earlier supporting his decision to bomb Vietnamese forces in Cambodia, a statement that drew the dissent of three Council members. In the depth of their feelings against communism, Meany and Nixon were bedfellows.

New York affairs were early entrants on the AFL-CIO agenda. Teachers in New York City went on strike in violation of a state law forbidding strikes by public employees. The union was fined $220,000, and Albert Shanker, who later became president of the national union, was sentenced to a term in prison. Governor Rockefeller announced that he would ask the state legislature to make the penalties for violation of the statute more severe. The Executive Council appropriated $100,000 to help the teachers.

A year later Nelson Rockefeller ran for reelection on the Republican ticket. His opponent was Arthur Goldberg, the former labor lawyer who had a distinguished career as Secretary of Labor, a member of the U.S. Supreme Court, and U.S. Ambassador to the United Nations. The New York State Federation of Labor, which Meany had once headed and in which the building trades had a strong representation, voted to endorse Rockefeller, the first time it had ever supported a Republican for governor. The endorsement was made by a standing vote of the delegates, and though all members of the AFL-CIO Executive Council, including eight pro-Goldberg members, agreed that the tally was accurate, it was decided to reconvene the state convention for another count. Some pro-Goldberg unions boycotted the convention, which re-endorsed Rockefeller.

Behind this unusual event was a history of favors to labor. Rockefeller promoted the expenditure of billions of dollars for public works, ensuring full employment for the building trades. Whenever a top union official retired and was given a dinner in his honor, Rockefeller turned up to present the gold watch. The unions were simply abiding by the Gompers precept of rewarding their friends, although the teachers may not have felt the same way.

AFFIRMATIVE ACTION

The aftermath of the struggle for civil rights brought some complicated employment problems to the fore. They were exemplified by a controversy over the so-called Philadelphia Plan. In a pilot project sponsored by the Department of Labor, bidders on government-financed projects were required to specify a "goal" of minority employment in certain skilled trades based upon the racial composition of the city's population. The AFL-CIO Building Trades Department offered an alternative scheme:

1. Acceleration and extension of an apprenticeship outreach program that had already been adopted.
2. A recommendation to local unions that they accept all qualified minority journeymen for a stated period of time.
3. Training programs for minority youths not yet of appropriate apprenticeship age.

The Philadelphia Plan was mandated despite this offer, and was denounced by the AFL-CIO as an illegal quota system. Meany declared:

Perhaps the biggest drawback of the Plan is that it diverts attention from the real, solid task of training and qualifying minority workers for a permanent place in the ranks of skilled workers on all construction work in an area, not just the federally-financed work. So I can say to you that we don't like this Plan. We feel it is political in nature. We feel that it was put forth on the basis of very poor information. We won't get in its way. We know it will fall of its own dead weight.[1]

A year after the Plan had been in effect, the Labor Department reported that on twenty-five federal projects in the Philadelphia area, 22 percent of those in the targeted crafts were minority workers, compared with a 2 percent minority membership in the unions concerned. The unions claimed that the minority employees had been drawn from the ranks of the local unions operating in the private sector and had not come from the outside. The Plan was extended to other cities despite union opposition. They argued that it was the contractors who kept minorities out of apprenticeship and limited their employment on construction jobs. The outreach programs did succeed in increasing minority participation in apprenticeships. Th Philadelphia Plan and its counterparts appear to have been effective in stimulating action by employers and unions.

Quotas came in for continual pounding by the unions. The 1973 AFL-CIO convention called them ''inherently undemocratic and, moreover, [they] serve as a cheap substitute for sound recruitment and training programs to enable minority members to upgrade themselves by achieving the skills necessary for better-paying and more secure employment.''[2] The condemnation of some government-promoted affirmative action was particularly strong when it threatened to interfere with the seniority system in determining the order of layoffs or discharges. ''The seniority system is a cornerstone of the American labor movement. It is a contractual right. Seniority itself is color blind. American workers, regardless of race or sex, must not be compelled by government to surrender a portion of the work to junior employees.''[3] The Executive Council committed itself to the support of valid efforts to protect seniority systems, and also opposed any forced work-sharing requirements.

Apart from employment, the Federation did support civil rights measures. The Kentucky State Federation of Labor complained that forced busing of children was tearing the Louisville labor movement apart. But an AFL-CIO convention resolved that ''we wholeheartedly support busing of children when it will improve the educational opportunities of children.''[4]

THE ECONOMY

In August 1971, President Nixon issued a proclamation under the Economic Stabilization Act freezing wages and prices for ninety-nine days to curb inflationary tendencies. Contractual cost-of-living adjustments were prohibited. Not all prices were frozen; eggs, fruits, and vegetables were exempted. No machinery was established to monitor prices, but employers could be counted on to hew to the line on wages.

A Cost of Living Council was appointed to oversee the program. A second phase came in October with the creation of a Pay Board including, *inter alia,* five labor members, three from the AFL-CIO and one each from the UAW and the Teamsters. After a great deal of skirmishing Nixon agreed that the Board would be autonomous and that its decisions and standards could not be appealed to the Cost of Living Council. This was a condition for labor participation. George H. Boldt, a federal judge from the state of Washington, was named chairman, plus four additional public members all of whom the unions considered pro-management.

Trouble was not long in coming. In one of its first rulings the Board held that wage increases contracted during the initial ninety-day freeze could not be paid, and it ruled that future contract increases could not exceed 5.5 percent. The ninety-day issue was resolved when Congress enacted legislation allowing these increases on the ground that the Board's ruling was retroactive. After several more Board decisions, one affecting a three-year contract in the aerospace industry and another the West Coast longshoremen, four labor members resigned, leaving only the Teamster representative. The reason they gave was that the Board was controlling wages inequitably while leaving profits untouched. Nixon denounced the resignations as selfish and reconstituted the Board on an entirely public basis.

When prices began to accelerate during the second half of 1972 there was a further revision of the program, dubbed phase three. Mandatory controls were largely abolished and voluntary compliance substituted. The Pay Board was dropped and a new bipartite Labor-Management Advisory Committee installed. In June 1973, Nixon instituted a sixty-day retail price freeze in preparation for phase four. At the same time he imposed export controls on soybeans, cottonseed, and feed grains in order to increase their domestic supply. Phase four represented still another attempt to stop the inflation, which was being fed by a large increase in oil prices, the first so-called oil shock. It placed more emphasis on such macroeconomic measures as a tighter money supply and a reduction of federal expenditures. This final phase was denounced as unfair to labor by the AFL-CIO, which called for an end to the entire stabilization program as soon as possible.

The remnants of the program continued in low gear with little labor participation. Soon after he replaced Nixon as President, Gerald Ford declared that controls were unworkable and unwise, and refused to maintain them depite the heightened inflation, which had risen from 6.2 percent in 1973 to 11 percent in 1974. To make matters worse, unemployment was also going up. This was a new economic phenomenon called stagflation. In the past, unemployment had generally been negatively correlated with inflation.

Attention turned to the alleviation of unemployment. Interest rates had risen, adversely affecting housing and other construction. Congress enacted a public works bill in May 1975, but Ford vetoed it. The Executive Council came up with a program entitled Get America Back to Work, with the following proposals:

1. An immediate tax cut of at least $20 billion.
2. Measures to reduce American dependence on imported oil and a system of rationing the available supply.
3. Reduced interest rates and allocation of credit for high-priority social and economic activities.
4. Massive federal efforts to create jobs through construction of roads, hospitals, and other infrastructure.
5. Revision of the structure of the Federal Reserve system to make it more responsive to the public.
6. Federal aid to state and local governments.
7. The protection of domestic jobs from unfair foreign competition.

There was no concern expressed about the creation of a federal deficit. In fact, Meany termed the congressional fear of deficits appalling. Congress enacted a tax cut of $25 billion in March 1975, which Ford signed while protesting that it was too large.

Stabilization and its aftermath did little to avert inflation, which had begun even before the oil price rise. The labor movement was a reluctant participant in the program to curb it; the unions would have preferred to stay out were it not for the fear that their interests would suffer did they not participate. There was particular opposition to wage controls lest collective bargaining be impaired. Their economic philosophy at the time reflects what they found wrong with the entire program: The proceedings of the 1977 convention state:

In addition to policies geared to the specific inflationary sectors of the economy, the foundation of any anti-inflationary program must be full employment. National economic policy must be directed toward full employment programs which reduce the inflationary pressure of under-utilized plant and equipment and wasted human resources. Overall budget decisions, the policies of the Federal Reserve Board, and specific programs aimed at problem areas can increase productivity and promote efficiency through full use of all resources. This approach offers a practical means to attack inflation. Wage and price controls or deliberately maintained high unemployment do not.[5]

Certain presidential actions served to increase union ire. When congressional attempts to modify the Davis-Bacon Act, which provided a mechanism for fixing wages on government-financed construction jobs, had failed, Nixon attempted to suspend its operation through the use of his national emergency powers. The outcry was so great that enforcement of the Act was reinstated and supplemented by a tripartite construction committee with the mandate of preventing excessive wage increases. Nixon instituted a six-month delay in pay raises for federal employees. For these and other actions, the AFL-CIO promised an all-out campaign against his reelection in 1972, a promise that was not kept.

SITUS PICKETING

A Supreme Court case decided in 1951 created a cause célèbre. A union representing striking skilled workers set up a picket line at the site of a construction job. It had been customary for all employees on a project to refuse to cross such picket lines, thus effectively tying up all work. The question that arose was whether using employers of other crafts on the project to increase pressure on the primary employer was a secondary boycott in violation of the Taft-Hartley Act. The Supreme Court held that it was and limited picketing to the off-site offices of the primary employer, thus greatly reducing the effectiveness of the strike.[6]

Reversing this doctrine became the principal legislative goal of the building trades. Their best chance came when John Dunlop became Ford's Secretary of Labor. Dunlop had worked particularly closely with construction industrial relations problems. With the agreement of Ford, he wrote a bill that would have permitted picketing at the site of a construction project, and sweetened it with provisions that reduced the power of local unions to enter into collective agreements without the moderating influence of their national unions. Both houses of Congress passed the bill by comfortable margins, but Ford vetoed it. In a later-written autobiography he acknowledged that he had committed himself to support the legislation, but that heavy pressure from employers, threatening to oppose his nomination for the presidency in the coming election, had dissuaded him.

In consequence, Dunlop resigned his cabinet post and Meany declared that "we in the labor movement believe a man's word is his bond. Now the President has shown what his word is worth." Ironically, if Ford had managed to gain the Republican nomination he would probably have won the presidential election. It was very close, and in the likely event that the building unions would have supported him he might have carried some key states that went for Carter, who had no particular relationship with the labor movement.

BARGAINING AND ORGANIZING

Collective bargaining was complicated by inflation and stabilization. One response to inflation was the proliferation of cost-of-living allowances in collective agreements. Efforts to strengthen job security in the face of rising unemployment took the form of work guarantees, attrition plans, new training programs, increases in severance pay, and reduced hours of work. There was increased emphasis on nonwage benefits to compensate for limitations on wages.

When the stabilization program ended in 1974, markedly higher wage settlements began to appear in agreements, but the onset of double-digit inflation reduced real wages. A favorable development for the unions was the enactment of the Employment Retirement Security Act (ERISA), a first step in preventing the erosian of pension rights. Had it not been for inflation, it would probably have been very difficult to induce Congress to take this step.

When the consumer price increase fell from 9 percent in 1975 to 6 percent in 1976, wage settlements also declined. Average real weekly take-home pay after taxes was virtually unchanged from 1969 to 1976, which in a way was a triumph for collective bargaining. The AFL-CIO was not hesitant in taking credit for this outcome: The Executive Council Report to the 1977 Convention states:

Union workers and their families have suffered as a result of the worst economic mess since the 1930s, but through the collective bargaining process, union members are catching up and protecting themselves from future hardship. . . . Real wages are beginning to improve after being eroded by inflation during the last ten years. During the last few years, collective bargaining has proved itself able to provide some protection for the American worker during these trying times of high unemployment and ever increasing costs.[7]

As for new organizing, the 1970s were marked by phenomenal growth of public sector unionization. The amalgamation of five unions of postal workers and their affiliation with the AFL-CIO brought in 300,000 new members. Recognition of the changing composition of the labor force and its requirements was reflected in an endorsement of a proposed equal rights amendment to the constitition, a position that the Federation had declined to take just a few years earlier. The four million women who had joined unions made the difference. The cooperative organizing plans continued, with some success. The Los Angeles program yielded 275,000 new members over its lifetime. Orlando-Tampa and New Orleans were added to the list of targeted cities.

Controversy developed over a convention resolution stating that public employees should have the same right to strike as those in the private sector. Jerry Wurf, whose union (the State, County, and Municipal Workers) was busy organizing in the public sector, offered an amendment to the effect that binding arbitration might substitute for strikes in the case of safety personnel, citing the need to preserve public order and the unwillingness of state legislatures to permit policemen and firemen to go out on strike. He believed that committing state governments to arbitration was a second best solution, and argued that public sector employees would never gain the right to strike if security personnel were included. To an old trade unionist, this was heresy; Meany intervened with the comment, "I hope I never see the day that the AFL-CIO sitting in convention will ask Congress to impose compulsory arbitration on anybody anywhere at any time." His wish was granted; the Wurf amendment was defeated.[8]

SOME SIDELIGHTS

What was later recognized as a gaffe was a letter sent by the Executive Council to Kurt Waldheim congratulating him on his election as general-secretary of the United Nations. However, compensation came in the form of an AFL-CIO banquet for the Soviet novelist Alexander Solzhenitsyn when President Ford declined to invite him to the White House for fear of offending the Russians. The distinguished author praised the Federation for its consistent anticommunist stance, which was demonstrated once more when the Executive Council supported the Longshoremen's union in embargoing grain shipments to the USSR. The union had demanded assurance that future grain sales would not lead to repetition of the concessional prices of 1972 that contributed to higher food prices in the United States. The embargo was suspended when President Ford agreed to send a representative to Moscow to negotiate a fair price rather than leaving it to individual sellers to do.

After his second inauguration, Nixon paid a visit to the Executive Council to thank it for supporting his Vietnam policy. In reshuffling his cabinet, Nixon appointed Peter J. Brennan to be Secretary of Labor. Brennan was the president of the New York City and State building trades councils, and had organized a pro-Nixon hard hat demonstration in New York. Moreover, nine construction unions had endorsed Nixon, and this was their reward. Subsequently, Meany denounced Brennan for testifying in favor of a proposed subminimum wage for young people. Nixon appeared at a meeting of the Building Trades Department to argue that the wage decision had been made by the cabinet as a whole and that Brennan simply went along as a team player. Meany's response was that Brennan was on the wrong team. No tears were shed at Federation headquarters when Brennan was forced to resign because of his involvement in a corruption investigation.

Despite a chaotic economy and a somewhat hostile political environment, the Federation and its constituent unions did rather well during the Nixon-Ford years. An opinion poll conducted by *US News and World Report* in 1976 ranked organized labor fourth among the most powerful institutions in the country, outranked only by the White House, the Supreme Court, and the television industry. Its affluence enabled the Federation to make a sizable investment in a new Institute for Labor Studies; a small college with a twenty-seven-acre campus located just outside the Washington beltway, with 130 beds in 100 guest rooms and a 200-seat auditorium, was purchased. AFL-CIO membership reached a peak of more than 14 million in 1975, due mainly to the influx of public employees. The fly in the ointment was the concomitant growth of the labor force, which dropped the density ratio from 16.1 percent in 1969 to 13.7 percent in 1977.

NOTES

1. Archie Robinson, *George Meany and His Times* (New York: Simon and Schuster, 1981), p. 291.

2. AFL-CIO, *Proceedings of the Tenth Constitutional Convention*, 1973, p. 233.

3. AFL-CIO, *Report of the Executive Council to the Eleventh Constitutional Convention*, 1975, p. 216.

4. AFL-CIO, *Proceedings of the Eleventh Constitutional Convention*, 1975, p. 261.

5. AFL-CIO, *Proceedings of the Twelfth Constitutional Convention*, 1977, p. 93.

6. *NLRB v. Denver Building Trades*, 341 U.S. 675 (1951).

7. AFL-CIO, *Report of the Executive Council to the Twelfth Constitutional Convention*, 1977, p. 123.

8. AFL-CIO, *Proceedings of the Eleventh Constitutional Convention*, 1975, p. 490.

CHAPTER 6

The Carter Interlude

The labor movement greeted the election of Jimmy Carter with satisfaction. George Meany declared:

The President we supported so strongly and so successfully in the last election brought into office a sense of hope and a spirit of inspiration that has brightened the land. He has shunned the negativism of the past two administrations, choosing to present to the Congress and the American people major programs for welfare, energy, illegal aliens, food stamps, minimum wage and labor law reform, among many.[1]

It was not long, however, before the unions discovered that the nirvana had not yet arrived.

The first difference that arose involved the selection of a secretary of labor. The AFL-CIO put forward the name of John Dunlop, who had performed yeoman work for it in the situs picketing affair. Much to its surprise, Carter nominated F. Ray Marshall, a little known professor at the University of Texas. The unions accepted this choice with grace, and Marshall turned out to be a friend. At his confirmation hearing before the Senate Labor Committee he made a good start by supporting practically everything on the labor agenda.

ECONOMIC POLICY

The principal issue of controversy between the AFL-CIO and the Carter administration was economic policy. Inflation had slowed to 5.8 percent by 1976, but it soon began to rise, reaching 13.5 percent in 1980. The specter of wage and price controls appeared again. The Federation had been through this situation once and had no inclination to try it again.

Early in his tenure Carter proposed an expenditure of $4 million for employment creation, stretched over two years, to reduce the rate of unemployment that was running over 7 percent. The Federation had lobbied for $10 million for the first year alone. Secretary-Treasurer Lane Kirkland expressed disappointment with the Carter economic program, particularly a proposed reduction in the corporate income tax. Carter's announcement that he planned to strengthen the Council on Wage and Price Policy, which he had inherited from President Gerald Ford, was not welcomed. Rumors of a plan to require unions and employers to give prior notice of wage demands and offers caused Meany to blow up:

We are absolutely opposed to it, completely opposed to it, even if Billy Carter wants it. We will oppose it. We will not cooperate. It would destroy collective bargaining. . . . This would destroy our flexibility at the bargaining table. . . . And actually, it's just a foot in the door—then the next thing is voluntary guidelines.[2]

Meany's pronouncement stopped the idea of controls for the moment.

The AFL-CIO had long been a supporter of minimum wage increases, and this seemed a good time to get one. When the administration proposed an increase from $2.30 to $2.50 an hour, the Federation termed it "shameful" and demanded $3.00. A Coalition for a Fair Minimum Wage was formed to put pressure on the administration, which agreed to support $2.65 for the first year and then to advance it in two annual steps to 53 percent of the average hourly factory wage. The House approved $2.65 effective January 1, 1978, plus two more annual steps to $3.05, but the bill that eventually cleared Congress provided for a step increase to $3.35 by 1981. This increase did not keep up with the inflation, and it was not a great victory for the unions.

On April 15, 1977, Carter called for voluntary cooperation by labor, management, and government to stop the inflation. A private labor-management group headed by Meany and Reginald Jones, president of General Electric, recommended working with the President on a broad range of economic policy issues but rejected controls or guidelines. The Federation challenged Carter's optimism on the pace of economic recovery and criticized him for abandoning the drive for more jobs.

Later in the year Meany was asked in a television interview what he thought of Carter's performance thus far. He replied:

I think the President is a conservative. I don't think he's quite as conservative as Ronald Reagan or quite as conservative as Gerald Ford or Nixon. . . . He wants to push the economy forward. My complaint is that he's not giving the attention to the real problem, the job problem [that] we expected he would. He seems to have some idea that his greatest accomplishment would be balancing the budget by 1981. . . . I'm not opposed to balancing the budget but what price do we pay in human terms?[3]

With consumer price increases running at a high level, Carter finally proposed that labor and business participate in a voluntary program to decelerate the pace of price and wage increases below the annual rate of the two previous years. The Executive Council rejected even voluntary guidelines. The labor members of the Federal Pay Council, an advisory body on the salaries of federal employees, resigned in protest against a proposal to limit their raises to 5.5 percent.

In another effort to control inflation, the administration, in October 1978, proposed a voluntary 7 percent cap on wage increases and a nonspecific price guideline. The Federation agreed that inflation had become the nation's number one problem and that remedial action was necessary, but it found the proposal unfair in that it concentrated on wages. There was no mechanism for adjusting wage inequities and no protection for low-wage workers. Collective bargaining would be impaired. The report of the Executive Council to the thirteenth convention stated:

While the program demonstrates the President's desire to address the problem of inflation, the plan his advisers have devised is unfair and inequitable and the end result of their ill-considered proposals could well be another recession, with mass unemployment, which at least one administration spokesman is already predicting.[4]

The Council made a counter-offer: It agreed to support a program that called for full controls of every source of income—profits, dividends, rents, interest rates, executive compensation, and professional fees—as well as wages and prices. This would be backed by detailed legislation, not simply a standby grant of authority to the President. Although the Executive Council was aware that the proposal had no chance of enactment, it was a way of showing that labor was willing to cooperate on a nondiscriminatory basis.

As on alternative to his earlier proposal, President Carter issued an executive order creating voluntary wage and price guidelines to be monitored by the Council on Wage and Price Policy. The AFL-CIO filed suit in a federal court asking that this order be enjoined on the ground that it was essentially mandatory in that firms could be barred from the award of federal contracts if they declined to accept it. A district court ruled that the President had exceeded his authority by attempting to institute controls through the procurement power of the government, but the Appeals Court reversed this decision and the Supreme Court denied review.

In an effort to repair the breakdown in the relationship between labor and the Carter administration, a so-called National Accord was reached on September 28, 1979, a broad document that covered the entire range of economic policy. Voluntary wage and price restraints were to be continued with provision for greater public participation. A tripartite advisory committee of 18 members was to devise appropriate wage standards.[5]

As one of its first acts, this Committee recommended a range of 7.5 to 9.5 percent for permissible wage increases. The new experiment in control had little effect. Consumer prices rose by 11.3 percent in 1979 and 13.5 percent in 1980.

After the 1980 elections, but before Ronald Reagan was inaugurated, the Committee recommended that the voluntary guidelines be permitted to lapse, on the ground that inflation was too high and administrative regulations too complex to command effective public support. Reagan terminated the entire scheme soon after he came into office.

These years of futile efforts to control inflation by government mandate ended with the defeat of Carter. Many believe that one of the principal reasons for his failure to be reelected was the magnitude of the inflation, one of the worst in American history. The second large oil price increase in 1979 was an important factor, but not the only one. A consequence was that a good part of the energies of the labor movement were diverted from other tasks. The transfer of power from Carter to Reagan was certainly not a desirable outcome from labor's point of view, despite its differences with President Carter and his economic advisers.

LEGISLATION

It was hoped that the situs picketing bill vetoed by Ford would have a better chance of enactment with a Democrat in the White House. Early in 1977, a House committee cleared relevant legislation, but a massive employer campaign resulted in its defeat in the full House by the close vote of 217–205. This campaign was directed by the National Right to Work Committee and the Associated General Contractors, the largest employer organization in construction. That laid the issue to rest for some years.

Another piece of legislation strongly backed by the Federation was one that dealt with labor law reform, designed in part to speed NLRB processing of representation elections and unfair labor practice charges. (This legislation is discussed in detail below.) The Executive Council set up a coordinating task force and voted a special assessment of one cent per member per month to finance its activities. A 22-minute color film entitled *Reform At Last*, supplemented by radio programs, leaflets, posters, and a weekly newspaper, were developed, one of the most comprehensive efforts ever undertaken by labor. As a result, this bill passed the House by the comfortable margin of 257–163.

Again there was tremendous opposition from major employer groups as well as individual corporations, including Sears Roebuck and Firestone Tire. When the Senate convened a few months after the House had acted, changes were made to satisfy doubtful senators; as a result, it was estimated that there were enough votes to obtain cloture, But the tally was 58–39, two votes short of the necessary sixty. Then each senator who had voted with the minority was asked what further changes were necessary to secure his vote. There was no give, and the bill was returned to committee, where it eventually died. The AFL-CIO was bitter. The report of the Executive Council to the thirteenth convention stated:

The failure was due to the fact that the business community stood silent or was the willing ally of those whose basest motives are either an emasculated labor movement or none at all. That is a failure that could bring the greater harm to the fabric of America than the failure of one legislative measure.[6]

A weakened version of the original Humphrey-Hawkins bill committing the country to full employment was enacted in 1979. It called for a 3 percent rate of inflation by 1983 and zero inflation five years later, with a target of 4 percent unemployment, a balanced budget, and fully competitive international trade. Labor rightly regarded it as a mere symbol with little substance, certainly no compensation for the failure of labor law reform. One proposal sponsored by the administration that the AFL-CIO did oppose was deregulation of the airlines. The Pilots union maintained that it would impair safety, lead to cutthroat competition, and threaten jobs. The consequences of this legislation are still in dispute.

OTHER MATTERS

On the collective bargaining front, there were constant complaints that controls were frustrating the bargaining process. Cost-of-living agreements became almost universal as a result of the inflation. Federal employees were among the major gainers as a result of restructuring government management. Two new bodies were created by the Civil Service Reform Act of 1978, replacing the Civil Service Commission that had administered labor relations for many years. The Office of Personnel Management became the employment manager and the Federal Labor Relations Authority was to act as a little NLRB. These changes gave federal employees some real bargaining rights for the first time, though the right to strike was not one of them.

In another step toward recognition of the changing composition of the labor force, the AFL-CIO set up a Department of Professional Employees, to which 26 unions affiliated. Among the new unions chartered were the Industrial Union of Police Associations, with 60,000 members, and the Federation of Professional Athletes, of which the main component was the National Football League Players Association. The Brotherhood of Sleeping Car Porters, A. Philip Randolph's base, was down to a thousand members and merged with the Railway and Airline Clerks.

It might have been anticipated that a friendly administration in Washington would facilitate union organization. However, increased employer resistance, manifested by a rise in unfair labor practice complaints, remained an obstacle. The principal membership gains were in health care, the public services, and retail and wholesale trade. Total AFL-CIO membership was almost unchanged, but the density ratio fell again. It may have been too short a time to test the proposition that government attitudes toward unions are a critical determinant of their growth or decline. The composition of administrative bodies and employer reactions change too slowly. Whatever the reasons, four years of Carter did little to change the downward trend of union strength.

George Meany announced to the 1979 AFL-CIO convention that he would not accept reelection to the presidency. He died the next year at the age of 85 after having held the top posts of the AFL and AFL-CIO for almost thirty years. With the possible exception of Samuel Gompers, no one contributed more than Meany to the shaping of the American labor movement. He tended to be dictatorial and very sure of the wisdom of his views, but he was a strong proponent of union democracy and civil rights. Apart from the Auto Workers episode, he managed to knit the AFL and the CIO together into a viable organization despite the long history of animosity between the two. He was a consummate politician and under his tutelage the AFL-CIO came to represent the kind of labor organization that was adapted to the American environment.

His successor, Lane Kirkland, came from a Southern background, enjoyed a college education, and became a ship's officer in the merchant marine. He was a member of the Masters, Mates, and Pilots Union, and after serving as an aide to Meany, was elected secretary-treasurer of the AFL-CIO. He was a professional rather than a blue-collar worker as his predecessors had been. He was only the fourth president of the central body of American labor, apart from a one-year interregnum in 1894–1895. Few labor organizations around the world have had comparable tenures of office for their top leaders.

NOTES

1. AFL-CIO, *Report of the Executive Council to the Twelfth Constitutional Convention*, 1977, p. 1.

2. Archie Robinson, *George Meany and His Times* (New York: Simon and Schuster, 1981), p. 360.

3. Ibid., p. 369.

4. AFL-CIO, *Report of the Executive Council to the Thirteenth Constitutional Convention*, 1979, p. 77.

5. The full text of the agreement can be found in AFL-CIO, *American Federationist* (October 1979), p. 1.

6. AFL-CIO, *Report of the Executive Council to the Thirteenth Constitutional Convention*, 1979, p. 131.

CHAPTER 7

The Reagan Years

The inauguration of Ronald Reagan marked the beginning of the most difficult period for organized labor since the early 1930s. The administration was tilted sharply toward employers, who took advantage of the opportunity to mount a powerful attack against the unions. The concept of a "union-free environment" gained currency. The unions were on the defensive in the legislature. The Carter regime, with all its tensions, seemed like a golden age in retrospect.

The unions fought back with new organizing techniques and programs designed to appeal to prospective members as consumers as well as beneficiaries of collective bargaining. Several unions in the service and public sectors grew rapidly, reflecting the changing composition of the labor force. But others in the traditional strongholds of organization, manufacturing in particular, were decimated by a combination of employer hostility and job loss. The net result was that AFL-CIO membership was almost the same in 1989 as in 1981, thanks to the reaffiliation of the Teamsters in 1987, but the labor force grew by 14 percent between these years, bringing the density ratio to a new low.

The first portent of things to come was the appointment of Raymond J. Donovan, a construction company executive from New Jersey, as Secretary of Labor. On the other hand, a private labor-management advisory group that had been established in 1973 was reconstituted, and the UAW voted to reaffiliate. These were hopeful signs.

THE PROFESSIONAL AIR TRAFFIC CONTROLLERS ORGANIZATION (PATCO)

The first real test of Reagan's intentions toward labor was the PATCO affair. Executive Order 10988 issued by President John F. Kennedy in 1962 and the

Civil Service Reform Act of 1978 had granted federal employees bargaining rights. After several months of negotiation between PATCO and the Federal Aviation Authority, an agreement was reached, subject to ratification by the union's members, raising pay for the 17,000 controllers by 11 percent, an average of $4,000 per person. This was more than other federal employees were getting, but it took into account the excessive pressures involved in demanding jobs. Six weeks later the contract was overwhelmingly rejected by 95 percent of PATCO members, who wanted more pay, early retirement, a shorter work week, and greater control of their equipment. A strike was called, to which 13,000 employees responded.

The union had begun planning for an eventual strike several years earlier because of the mounting frustrations of the controllers. It was almost committed to a strike if all its demands were not met. There had been less widespread work stoppages by federal employees in the past that were settled by mediation, and it was expected that this would happen once again. Instead, Reagan issued a back-to-work ultimatum in which all employees who were not on the job in 48 hours were threatened with discharge, an action within his authority under the Taft-Hartley Act. Some 11,500 controllers were discharged when they refused to obey this order and their union was decertified as their bargaining agent.[1]

This was a completely unexpected course of events. Law or no law, this was not the way similar controversies had been settled in the past. There was a famous precedent of which Reagan was aware and may have influenced him: in 1919, the Boston police force went on strike and when a similar threat by a little known governor of Massachusetts, Calvin Coolidge, was ignored, the entire police force was discharged and a new one recruited. Much to the surprise of the controllers, the planes were kept flying by nonstrikers, supervisors, and military controllers until a sufficient number of replacements could be trained.

Reagan made it clear by throwing down the gauntlet that labor relations were in for a change under his administration. The labor movement was outraged, to put it mildly. A group of Executive Council members met with him to urge that the controllers be reinstated, but he refused, although he agreed that they could apply for other federal employment. This was not much of a concession, since the government was not hiring. Eventually, PATCO went into bankruptcy. It was not until a later transportation act lifted the ban on airport rehiring of the strikers that unionism returned to the industry. A new National Air Traffic Controllers Union, chartered as an affiliate of the Marine Engineers, won a representation election by a two-to-one margin.

FEDERAL APPOINTMENTS

The AFL-CIO spent a good deal of time testifying against nominees to federal posts. One of the first was John van de Water, who was nominated to the chairmanship of the NLRB and who had been a management consultant giving advice on fending off unionism. When the Senate turned him down, the White

House nominated Donald Dotson, a management labor relations lawyer. The AFL-CIO decided not to oppose him because his record was not unduly hostile, a decision they later had cause to regret. They eventually charged Dotson with failure to enforce the law and to have engineered major reversals of Board doctrine, facilitating unfair labor practices by employers. A study of NLRB decisions during the first year he served as chairman showed that 60 percent of contested unfair labor practice and representation cases were decided in favor of employers, compared with 27 percent under Ford and 29 percent under Carter.

The Federation expressed concern over the nomination of Rosemary Collier as NLRB general counsel, a key administrative position. She was given a recess appointment after the Senate failed to act on her nomination. Donald J. Devine was opposed as director of the Federal Office of Personnel Management on the ground that he had impeded collective bargaining. He withdrew his name from consideration when confirmation appeared unlikely. The unions added their voice to the successful campaign against the confirmation of Robert H. Bork to the U.S. Supreme Court.

There was a running battle with the Labor Department under Donovan. He was charged with representing the interests of employers against unions, with filling key positions with antiunionists, and with reducing funds designed for worker protection, notably the budget of the Occupational Safety and Health Administration. Another issue of contention involved homework, which had been forbidden in six apparel-related trades to prevent violation of the Fair Labor Standards Act. The Department first attempted to lift the ban in 1981, and persisted until 1988, when the ban was finally lifted. Although employers were required to register with the Department to receive certificates of compliance, to the unions it was "a green light to exploit workers."

Donovan was indicted for grand larceny and fraud in 1984 in connection with a New York construction project, and had to resign. His successor was William E. Brock, the U.S. trade representative for the the preceding four years and a former U.S. senator. He left the Department a few years later to run Robert Dole's campaign for the Republican presidential nomination. He was one of the few Reagan appointees for whom the Federation had kind words. After he had addressed the 1987 AFL-CIO convention, stressing the important role of labor in furthering American democracy, Lane Kirkland called him a man of integrity and ability who would be missed. His successor was Anne Dore McLaughlin, who had been undersecretary in the Interior Department and who had almost no experience in labor matters.

LEGAL ACTIVITIES

Various past Republican administrations had attempted to induce Congress to repeal or modify the Davis-Bacon Act, the law that nonunion construction contractors disliked above all others. Another tack was tried in 1982 when the Labor Department changed the administrative rules to permit the substitution of semiskilled for skilled workers (two helpers for every three journeymen) and tightened the definition of prevailing wages to weaken the effectiveness of the Act. The Building Trades Department went to court and secured a temporary injunction blocking the new regulations. This was made permanent on the grounds that the Department could not simply overturn half a century of administrative precedents without making a strong showing that the intent of Congress had been misinterpreted over the years. However, a Court of Appeals reinstated the new regulations, and the Supreme Court declined to review. The building unions did support an administration proposal to amend the Act by trimming its coverage but strengthening its enforcement. The contract threshhold was raised from $2,000 to $25,000 for new construction, although the administration had been seeking a $100,000 limit. On the whole, the building trades survived fairly well this latest attempt to emasculate Davis-Bacon.

A legal development of some concern to the unions was the use of bankruptcy proceedings by employers to rid themselves of collective agreements. Congress was persuaded in 1984 to enact legislation barring this device, labor's sole legislative victory. Employers were required thenceforth to bargain in good faith over contract changes they wanted to make as part of the reorganization process. Behind this legislation were the activities of Frank Lorenzo, who employed bankruptcy as a means of breaking off relations with the Pilots union.

A similar problem arose in connection with leveraged corporate takeovers, sometimes with the same results for collective agreements. By January 1989, the known loss of union jobs traceable to mergers reached 90,000. Discussion at the 1985 AFL-CIO convention made clear what the unions thought of this practice:

The corporate merger is a disgrace. The leveraged buyouts [sic] that's going on in this country are a disgrace and lay it at the door of the person responsible. The Reagan Administration is responsible. He permitted the big mergers of the oil companies and now anyone that wants to merge can merge.[2]

To prevent this, the Executive Council recommended the strengthening of penalties for insider trading; making tender offers fairer for stockholders by requiring that they vote on proposed mergers; and the prevention of collusive sales of assets to incumbent management. Collective agreements, it was urged, should be made binding on corporate successors; and tapping pension funds should be prohibited. There should be no golden parachutes to bribe premerger management. No legislation was forthcoming.

The Federation did play an important role in the enactment of a law requiring advance notice of proposed layoffs. As originally passed by the House, when a firm planned to dismiss at least 50 people in the course of shutting down a plant or office, 180 days notice would have been required if it were a large employer and 90 days for small ones. This was watered down by the Senate to 60 days for all. Reagan was against the Act, but he did not veto it, and it became law without his signature. Notice was not required if the layoff was caused by "not reasonably foreseeable" circumstances; if providing notice adversely affected a firm's ability to raise capital or attract new business; or if a strike were in progress.

This was a small step in the direction of stopping the fairly common situation of a plant shutting down without any advance warning whatsoever. The qualifications for the requirement made it easy to avoid notification. A recent study concluded that:

the legislation has had at most a small impact on the provision of notice of the length stipulated under the Act. This non-event is at least partially due to the liberal firm-size and layoff threshholds for determining coverage under WARN.[3]

The AFL-CIO had long sought to regularize immigration and to prevent the employment of aliens in the United States, particularly in agriculture. As a result of these efforts, legislation was enacted in 1986 under which, for the first time, employers could be penalized for knowingly hiring illegal aliens. The so-called *bracero* program was tightened by requiring employers to secure a visa for each seasonal worker admitted to the United States and to apply to the Labor Department for certification that the employment of aliens would not adversely affect the working conditions of American workers doing similar jobs. A government commission appointed to assess the operation of the law reported in 1992 that its failings "are most important in agriculture. . . . The migrant and seasonal farm labor force is the easiest place for illegal immigrants to find work, and agriculture, especially labor-intensive fruit and vegetable farming, is the industry most dependent on them."[4]

An analysis of the union legislative record during Reagan's first term concluded that the unions weathered the period without any substantial defeats. They tended to do well in the House but lose out in the Senate. They were weakest in the area of administrative regulation. Reagan appointees, the NLRB in particular, made decisions that were detrimental to them.[5] Much the same conclusion would apply to the second term as well.

INTERNAL DEVELOPMENTS

There were some significant structural changes during the period. The independent National Association of Government Employees, with 80,000 members—half in the federal service, 20,000 employed by state and local governments, and 20,000 police officers—joined the Service Employees Union. Some 21,000 air flight attendants broke away from the Pilots union and received their own charter. The West Coast Longshoremen, long a pariah since its withdrawal from the CIO because of its communist leadership, finally affiliated with the AFL-CIO. The big event was the reaffiliation of the Teamsters after thirty years of a separate and stormy existence. When Jackie Presser, the Teamster president whose record as a union official was far from unblemished, came to the podium of a Federation convention to announce that the union was coming back in, he received a standing ovation. This was presumably not a personal encomium, but rather a reflection of the fact that he brought almost 1.4 million members with him.

The perennial problem of the state and central local bodies was once more on the agenda. Efforts to force affiliates to join the Federation had been uniformly unsuccessful. A plan was devised in 1987 wherby unions that elected to do so would pay the AFL-CIO a monthly affiliation fee on behalf of its members equal to 75 percent of the average levied by the various central bodies. It was hoped that this bargain rate would encourage support for the centrals.

The combination of recession and Reagan policies made the first half of the 1980s lean years for organization of new members. The Executive Council noted that "employer opposition to actual and incipient organizing campaigns had reached epidemic proportions." One campaign that received a great deal of publicity involved the Hotel and Restaurant union, which won a contract for 3,000 white-collar workers employed by Yale University. A strike of professional football players that received more national attention that any strike in recent years—except perhaps the PATCO strike—did not end as well. Replacements were brought in and the strikers were barred from playing for the rest of the season.

To prevent costly duplication of organizing, the Executive Council devised a plan similar to that used to resolve jurisdictional disputes. Mediation and arbitration were to be employed to designate organizing jurisdiction, a scheme already in effect in the building trades. After eighteen months of operation twenty-eight cases had been filed, fourteen were settled by mediation, and the rest decided by umpires. The program made unions more selective in seeking targets, more careful in estimating their chances of success, and more willing to participate in cooperative campaigns. For example, when the long boycott against the Coors Brewing Company was lifted, the Machinists, Steelworkers, and UAW began organizing. Through the good offices of the AFL-CIO, the two latter unions stepped back, leaving the way clear for the Machinists.

A new organizing technique that is discussed in greater detail below was inaugurated. Tactics either complementing or supplementing traditional campaigns were employed to expand the scope of disputes. Pressure was put on management through stockholders or financial institutions that dealt with the targeted firm. The public was involved by more sophisticated advertising designed to denigrate the firm's image. As the Executive Council wrote,

this strategy moves the issue beyond the closed-door privacy of the bargaining session to the general public, the executive board rooms of those serving on the company's board of directors, to those who lend it money and who buy its products, the regulatory agencies of federal, state, and local governments, and even overseas.[6]

The 1980s also marked more attention to the organization of women. Although women represented 28 percent of union membership in 1981, female unionists constituted only 15 percent of all women workers. Affiliates were urged to support the Coalition of Labor Union Women, a new group, and to make child care a major objective. However, caution was expressed about job evaluation litigation, which had aroused a great deal of controversy. Diana Rock, director of women's rights for the State County union, explained why: "What pay equity is not is a system where wages are set by courts, where men's salaries are lowered to achieve pay equity, and where new bureaucracies are necessary to implement the law."[7]

TRAINING

The Comprehensive Employment and Training Act of 1973 was the first attempt to pull together a number of federally financed training programs operated by the states. It was designed mainly to create public service jobs and its net impact was small. The Job Training and Partnership Act of 1982 terminated public service employment and provided block grants to the states. It was administered by private local industry councils of twenty-five members on the average, at least 51 percent of whom were drawn from business enterprises, half from small firms. The rest came from a variety of organizations, including unions and educational institutions. The emphasis was on disadvantaged workers, although a small portion of the funds was allocated to those who had been laid off because of industrial restructuring. The Economic Dislocation and Worker Adjustment Assistance Act of 1988 provided for more assistance to the latter group.

The unions were critical of these programs because of administrative shortcomings. They felt that it was wrong to pay subsidies to employers, which was done under the various laws. The Oregon Labor Council proposed in 1985 that the entire program be abandoned, and although the AFL-CIO did not back this initiative, it reflected union attitudes. The Executive Council decried the business domination of local councils as well as the lack of income support during training. It made a suggestion for improving the system: "The U.S. Employment Service must become the recognized, adequately financed source of free, employment related services for all workers who need jobs and for all employers who need workers."[8] Based upon European experience, this was a virtual necessity if training and employment were to be linked, but the recommendation passed unnoticed in Washington.

THE CHANGING SITUATION OF WORKERS AND THEIR UNIONS

In 1983, the AFL-CIO undertook an extensive examination of the problems confronting it. The Council established a committee on the evolution of work and its implications, chaired by Secretary-Treasurer Thomas Donohue, with the mandate of determining and responding to the changes that were taking place in the labor force and the working environment. The committee prepared an exceedingly interesting report, the title of which appears as the heading of this section. It was printed as a pamphlet and distributed in thousands of copies. There was no attempt to gild the lily. Union shortcomings were stated objectively and suggestions made for overcoming them. Below is a summary of the report's contents.

1. *The change in the workforce.* The decline of employment in unionized sectors of the economy as well as its growth in poorly organized sectors was stressed. Manufacturing and construction accounted for 50 percent of AFL-CIO membership but employed only 22 percent of the civilian labor force. The service industries were expected to employ almost three-quarters of the labor force by 1990, but less than 10 percent of those were organized and only 20 percent of AFL-CIO members were in unions that represented mainly service workers.

The growth of the workforce was concentrated largely in unorganized geographic areas, with California, Texas, and Florida getting the lion's share. In the two latter states only 12 percent of workers were unionized, the third and fourth lowest proportion in the country. Two-earner families were becoming the model, with at least one member working part time. Employment in unstable industries had grown rapidly but those employed there were often classified as independent contractors, managers, or supervisors to eliminate the possibility of organization.

2. *The failure of the law.* The report outlines the failure of the courts, the NLRB, and the federal government to provide protection for the statutory right to organize. This subject is dealt with below.

3. *The desires and perceptions of workers.* A number of opinion polls conducted over the previous quarter of a century were summarized. While 51 percent of nonunion workers expressed satisfaction with their jobs, only 40 percent were satisfied with their fringe benefits and 28 percent with their pay and opportunities for advancement. Over three-quarters of all workers—and the same percentage of nonunionists—agreed that unions improved wages and working conditions. More than 80 percent believed that unions were needed to help secure legitimate demands, yet 53 percent of nonunionists believed that wages and fringe benefits would not improve if their firms were organized. This contradiction was also reflected in the finding that while 60 percent thought their employers could raise wages without raising prices, more than half believed that employers were providing all the pay and benefits they could afford.

An important finding was that nonunionists did not think that unions were pursuing an agenda in line with their needs. Sixty-five percent believed that unions forced members to go along with policies they did not like, and 63 percent thought that union leaders, not members, decided on strikes. Fifty-four percent believed that unionism increased the risk of companies going out of business, 57 percent that unions stifled individual initiative, and 52 percent that they prevented necessary change.

Many of the responses of the union members who were queried were positive. They appreciated the benefits of unionization: Over 90 percent answered that unions improved wages and conditions of work; 67 percent rejected the proposition that unions were not essential to fair treatment; and 60 percent thought that their wages and benefits would be lower if their employer were not organized. They were better educated than the general population: Only 16 percent did not have a high school education, compared with 28 percent for the labor force; and 39 percent (versus 33 percent) had some college education or a degree. Their incomes were substantially higher than the overage for the entire labor force, and a larger proportion held white-collar jobs. Another 20 percent were craftsmen or foremen.

The report cited the Canadian experience, where the percentage of organization rose from 30 to 40 percent between 1963 and 1983, and attributed this to the fact that the Canadian government ''has not defaulted in its obligation to protect the right of self-organization.''

RECOMMENDATIONS OF THE REPORT

1. Unions should experiment with new approaches to representation and address new issues of concern to workers. Arbitration or mediation might be a substitute for stronger economic methods. Women are more concerned with the question of equal pay, and safety and health might be stressed. There was a hesitant suggestion in the Report about increased worker participation in making business decisions, coupled with the warning that quality-of-work programs might lead to a speedup of work if not properly supervised.

2. Consideration should be given to new categories of membership for employees in an unorganized unit. The survey data revealed that 28 percent of nonunion employees had been union members in the past, and that many more had voted for unions in unsuccessful organizing campaigns. These people might be interested in some type of membership.

3. The AFL-CIO should study the possibility of providing direct services and benefits outside the collective bargaining structure.

4. Unions should expand their use of the electronic media.

5. Comprehensive corporate campaigns and the pressure of public opinion should be used to secure the neutrality of employers whose employees seek to organize, as well as to assure good faith bargaining.

6. Members should be urged to participate in union activities through community services and better communication. They should be encouraged to follow convention proceedings and participate in conferences. Officers should use more occasions to address their members directly. Orientation courses for new members and leadership training should be strengthened.

7. Organizing activities should be improved by implementing the following

suggestions. Organizers require more thorough training, and should be recruited from both within and outside the labor movement. Targets should be chosen more carefully and polling data used to determine whether the time is ripe for organization. Labor conditions are apt to be worse for the 35 percent of the national labor force working in companies with fewer than twenty-five employees, and there is less likely to be strong resistance to organization in these smaller firms. There is a caveat: Servicing small units tends to be expensive and requires more attention. Efforts should be made to attract employees in organized bargaining units who have not joined a union; there are two million people in this category. "Every effort should be made to turn them from free riders to full and enthusiastic members."

8. Structural change to enhance the labor movement's overall effectiveness is a delicate subject in the committee report because it involves autonomy as well as internal operating procedures. The Executive Council is urged to adopt guidelines for prospective mergers. Fifty affiliated unions had under fifty thousand members, and an additional thirty, under one hundred thousand. Many of them had financial problems. Mergers are most likely to be effective where there is an overlap in industries covered, where a substantial proportion of members are in vertically integrated industries, and where members work for a common conglomerate. The Council has followed this suggestion by recommending mergers where there is a shared community of interest based on the industry of employment. In order to be considered a community of interest, the report states that "an affiliate either should have at least 20 percent of its members employed in that industrial category or its members in that category should constitute at least 20 percent of the total AFL-CIO members therein." This is by no means an exclusive definition; a community of interest could be demonstrated in other ways.

Several additional recommendations covering the resolution of organizing disputes and ways of funding state and local central bodies have also been acted upon by the Executive Council, as noted above.

UNION PRIVILEGE BENEFIT PROGRAMS

The recommendation to provide services outside the regular bargaining structure was approved by the 1985 convention. The benefits eventually offered were the following:

1. *Credit cards.* This proved to be the most popular benefit. By 1994, 2.25 million union members had received the union Master Card. A "starter" program extended credit to members who had no prior credit history and might have difficulty in securing cards through ordinary channels.
2. *Legal services.* A panel of more than 800 firms was prepared to provide free initial consultations, free follow-up phone calls and letters, and reduced rates for further services.

3. *Insurance.* Life insurance supplementing employer-paid insurance could be secured at 25 percent below the market rate. A unique feature was a waiver of premiums for those who were laid off or were participating in a union-sanctioned strike. More than 300,000 members had signed up for accident insurance outside the workplace.

4. *Mortgage and real estate services.* These were designed to help union members obtain financing for the purchase of a home and to assist them in buying and selling homes. By 1994, some $700 million in mortages had been provided to union members, who could also sell homes at concessional brokers' commissions. Every mortgage contained a strike protection benefit, and a welfare fund was available to help members meet their mortgage payments if they were locked out, laid off, or disabled.

Other benefits offered were a full service motor club, a buying network that provided price information, purchase discounts on the basis of union cards, a discount pharmacy service, and a personal loan program. The AFL-CIO is very high on this assortment of benefits, but what is not clear is the extent to which it has promoted the retention of old members and the attraction of new ones.

UNION YES

In response to another recommendation contained in the report, the Federation launched a massive advertising campaign in 1988, designed to improve its image, using the slogan "America Works Best When We Say Union YES." Thirteen million dollars were appropriated for this purpose. Brief commercials were linked to high-rated television programs featuring members from different walks of life who explained why they joined unions. All union publications received special ads. Contests were sponsored, union football players were sometimes featured. This was the first time that organized labor used modern advertising techniques to sell its services.

The spurt of union activity toward the close of the Reagan era reflected growing concern with the decline in membership and influence. It represented some hard thinking about possibilities for the future and optimism that the negative trends could be reversed once a less hostile government atmosphere was installed. Unfortunately for the unions, four more years of adversity were ahead before the various initiatives could be tested in a friendlier environment.

NOTES

1. For an account of the events surrounding the negotiations and the strike, see Herbert B. Northrup, "The Rise and Decline of PATCO," *Industrial and Labor Relations Review*, vol. 37, no. 2, (1984), pp. 167–184; Richard W. Hurd and Jill K. Krisky, "Communications," *Industrial and Labor Relations Review*, vol. 40, no. 1 (1986), pp. 115–127.

2. AFL-CIO, *Proceedings of the Sixteenth Constitutional Convention*, 1985, p. 127.

3. John T. Addison and McKinsey Blackburn, "The Worker Adjustment and Retrain-

ing Notification Act,'' *Industrial and Labor Relations Review*, vol. 47, no. 4 (1994), p. 650.

4. *New York Times*, October 23, 1992.

5. Marick F. Masters and John Thomas Delaney, ''Union Legislative Records During Reagan's First Term,'' *Journal of Labor Research* (Winter 1987), pp. 15–16.

6. AFL-CIO, *Report of the Executive Council to the Seventeenth Constitutional Convention*, 1987, p. 86.

7. AFL-CIO, *Proceedings of the Sixteenth Constitutional Convention*, 1985, p. 358.

8. AFL-CIO, *Report of the Executive Council to the Seventeenth Constitutional Convention*, 1987, p. 162.

CHAPTER 8

The Bush Years

The four years of the Bush administration saw little change in the fortunes of the labor movement. The economy was weak during the last two years, although unemployment had fallen somewhat. However, inflation exceeded that of all but the first two Reagan years. AFL-CIO membership was greater in 1991 than in 1987, and the density ration rose. This was by courtesy of the Teamsters Union; without their reaffiliation density would have continued to fall.

The first personnel appointment of interest to labor was that of Elizabeth Dole, the wife of Senator Robert Dole, to the post of Secretary of Labor. She was described by the *AFL-CIO News* as a person of proven stature and wide experience in public life. In introducing her at an AFL-CIO convention, Lane Kirkland stated that working relations with her had been open, cordial, and sometimes fruitful. When she was replaced in 1991 by Lynn Martin, who had served in the House of Representatives for ten years, the reception was not as cordial. Martin had a poor Committee on Political Education (COPE) voting record, and the Communications Workers canceled her invitation to attend their convention because she had announced that she would recommend a presidential veto if a striker replacement bill were enacted by Congress. The nomination of Clarence Thomas to the Supreme Court was opposed by the Federation on the basis of his record on the Civil Rights Commission.

LEGISLATION

The Federation fared no better in its legislative activities under George Bush than under Reagan. There was the usual struggle over the minimum wage, occasioned by persistent Congressional unwillingness to tie the minimum to the rate of inflation. Congress did vote to raise the minimum in 1989 from $3.35

an hour to $4.55 over a three-year period. It also introduced a modification that would have permitted employers to pay 85 percent of the minimum to newly hired workers for the first 60 days of their employment. Bush vetoed the bill, and Congress sent him another raising the minimum to $4.25 by 1991, including a ninety-day, 85 percent training wage for teen-agers in their first jobs, limited to one-quarter of an employer's labor force at any one time; this was signed by the President.

The unions were less successful in pushing through a so-called Family Leave Act, which would have required a period of unpaid leave to employees after the birth or adoption of a child or during the serious illness of a family member. After several tries, Congress finally enacted such a bill in 1991, only to have it vetoed.

The legislation that was top priority for the unions involved striker replacement. According to interpretations of labor laws by the courts and the NLRB, striking employees could be replaced permanently if an employer succeeded in recruiting other workers, provided the strike was not caused by the employer's unfair labor practice. This had become an increasingly common occurrence during the 1980s—a very effective device for ousting unions.

Legislation was introduced in 1990 to prevent this practice. Called the Workplace Fairness Act, it was passed by the House by a margin of 247–182. The AFL-CIO mounted a major campaign on its behalf, including testimony before Congress by a number of workers who had lost their jobs. Half a million dollars were spent on radio and television commercials. Almost a million letters and postcards flooded Capitol Hill offices. Polls indicated that two-thirds of the general public were opposed to permanent replacement.

There was a long discussion of the problem at the 1991 AFL-CIO convention, where William Bywater of the Electrical Workers declared that it was a matter of life or death for the labor movement. "Unless we get this legislation passed the union movement is going to go downhill like it has been going downhill for the past twelve years." Lynn Williams of the Steelworkers provided a case in point. Seventeen hundred workers at the Ravenswood Aluminum Company in West Virginia had been on strike for more than a year. Only twenty-two had crossed the picket line. The average age of those striking was 52 years, and the average length of service with the company, 22 years. The company had been taken over by a financier named Marc Rich who was living in Switzerland because of legal difficulties in the United States. Replacements had been secured almost as soon as the strike was called. Other companies cited for similar practices were International Paper, Eastern Airlines, Greyhound Bus, and the *New York Daily News*. A resolution adopted by the convention stated in part:

By first insisting on—and then implementing regressive bargaining positions, the employer can provoke a strike and then hire a new and more pliant scab workforce to permanently replace "the one that had the temerity to fight back."[1]

Despite all the efforts of the unions, the Senate failed by three votes to invoke cloture, saving President Bush the task of vetoing any bill that came out. Bill Clinton campaigned in 1992 as a supporter of the legislation, which put the unions squarely on his side.

THE AIRLINES

Airline deregulation led to heightened competition and put a great deal of pressure on wages. The way was cleared for entrepreneurs to enter the industry by founding new airlines or taking over existing ones. One of the most aggressive was Frank Lorenzo, whose name became a synonym for antiunionism.

Lorenzo started with a small carrier, Texas Air, and acquired Eastern Airlines in 1986. He demanded wage cuts to make Eastern more profitable, leading to a strike by 8,000 machinists whose picket lines were honored by the pilots and flight attendants. The machinists offered to submit the controversy to binding arbitration, but Lorenzo refused. The National Mediation Board recommended to Bush that he invoke a 60-day strike delay and appoint a board of inquiry to look into the matter, but he declined to do so, whereupon the House voted to set up a four-member commission to investigate and make recommendations in forty-five days. The Senate followed suit, but Bush vetoed the legislation.

The strike was supported by AFL-CIO unions to the tune of $1.89 million. The Federation's entire field staff coordinated a Stand Up to Lorenzo Day, and among other demonstrations was a march from Miami to Washington. Lorenzo took Eastern into bankruptcy, planning to sell off its assets—the profitable New York-Washington shuttle was sold—and run it on a stripped-down, nonunion basis. Congress passed legislation urging the bankruptcy court to have the airline resume operations under an impartial trustee. The Senate vote of 94–0 precluded a veto, and a trustee was appointed—with Lorenzo out of the picture. Unfortunately, this did not solve the problem. Eastern had been so weakened that it closed down on January 18, 1991, twenty-three months after the strike had begun. It had been flying for 62 years, one of the oldest airlines in the country. It left behind large debts, and thousands of good jobs were lost. The whole affair was an unmitigated disaster.

Another venerable airline, Pan American, ran into economic difficulties in 1991. Most of its operations were taken over by Delta Airlines in an attempt to restructure it. A few months later it, too, went out of business, stranding 8,000 employees.

Of the 17 airlines formed after deregulation, 14 were no longer operating by the end of 1991. Of the older carriers, Eastern, Braniff, and Pan American were gone, while TWA and Continental were in bankruptcy. The Transportaion Department of the AFL-CIO laid the disintegration of the industry directly at the door of the Airline Deregulation Act that had been sponsored by President Jimmy Carter. Analysts are still arguing about the proximate cause, but the AFL-CIO had no doubts about where responsibility should be placed.

STRATEGIC APPROACHES

The Executive Council created a Strategic Approaches Committee in 1989, charged with the development of a unified program to help individual unions that were locked in difficult disputes with employers. Among those in which it intervened, in addition to the Eastern Airlines strike, were actions against the Greyhound Lines and the *New York Daily News.*

The Amalgamated Transit Union asked for the committee's assistance a week before its contract with Greyhound expired. Management had proposed wage increases tied to productivity, unlimited contracting out, and benefit cuts for newly hired workers. More than nine thousand employees went on strike and twenty-one cities were designated major strike locations. After the strike had run for several months the union offered an unconditional return to work under the terms of the expired contract. Greyhound instead recruited strikebreakers and offered to take back fifty strikers. The Federation launched a corporate campaign which included finding a potential buyer for the company. After a year of the strike and faced with a nationwide boycott, Greyhound went into bankruptcy.

It eventually emerged in a much weakened condition and signed an agreement with the Transit union with a six-year duration, a 20 percent wage increase over the life of the contract, $22 million in back pay for the strikers, reinstatement of 200 drivers who had been discharged for alleged misconduct, and the ultimate recall of 530 employees in order of seniority. However, the strike was hardly a victory for the union. The work force was down to 3,500, and 2,000 replacements remained in their jobs. The rest of the union members were placed on a waiting list for recall when vacancies occurred. Greyhound's future is still far from secure.

A widely publicized strike was mounted against the *New York Daily News* in 1990. Ten unions were involved; they initially continued working after their contract had expired. The company announced that it was terminating the contract, including a dues checkoff provision. When several employees walked out to protest a personnel action they were informed that they were being permanently replaced. The strategic committee of the AFL-CIO coordinated strike activities and began a corporate campaign against the Tribune Company, the paper's owner. The newspaper's circulation fell from 1.1 million to 300,000, with most of its well-known feature writers gone, and it was forced into bankruptcy. Finally, after a strike that lasted 146 days, the paper was bought by Robert Maxwell, the press tycoon, who settled the dispute.

Other employers with which the committee became involved during the Bush years were the *Pittsburgh Press*, the Frontier Hotel in Las Vegas, the City of Philadelphia, the Bituminous Coal Operators Association, the Los Angeles teachers, and the Hood Furniture Company of Jackson, Mississippi. On the basis if its experience, the committee recommended the following guidelines for allocating Federation resources in the future:

1. The disputes should be of vital importance to the unions involved.

2. The disputes should be of strategic importance not only to the unions involved, but to the labor movement as a whole.

3. There should be a high likelihood that committee action will have a material impact on the outcome of the dispute.

4. The affiliated union involved should have committed adequate staff and financial resources to the dispute.

EMPLOYEE STOCK OWNERSHIP PLANS (ESOPS)

These schemes, promoted by employers, came into vogue in the 1980s. They were stimulated by legislation permitting a corporation to deposit its stock in a trust fund for the benefit of its employees and take a tax deduction of up to 15 percent per annum of the compensation earned by the beneficiaries. Banks that lent money to retirement funds to enable them to buy the stock could deduct half the interest they received from such loans from their gross income. Employees received stock in proportion to their incomes, with distributions to begin after retirement or separation from the firm. The stock was generally voted by the trustees, not the employee-owners.

The trade unions had mixed attitudes toward these schemes. They were a form of benefit, but the slogan of the promoters, every man a capitalist, suggested that they might contain some measure of antiunionism. The Executive Council set up a committee to advise unions on a proper course of action. At a seminar on ESOPS, Secretary-Treasurer Thomas Donohue warned that "employee ownership is like fire. It can keep us warm and cook our food, or it can destroy our homes and burn us badly. It depends on why it is used, how well it is controlled, and who is in charge."[2] Among the plan's proponents were the airline pilots, but they were interested primarily in the prospect of employees becoming majority stockholders.

INTERNAL AFFAIRS

The ranks of the AFL-CIO were augmented in 1989 by the return of the United Mine Workers. When this union left the AFL in 1947, its redoubtable leader, John L. Lewis, simply sent a note to the president of the AFL saying "Green. We resign. Lewis." When Lewis left the helm the union suffered corrupt leadership for some years but was eventually rescued by a young lawyer, Richard L. Trumka. However, at the time of its reaffiliation it was down to 80,000 members, a shadow of the organization that had financed the CIO. Now all the major unions in the country were back in the unified central body of organized labor, with the exception of the largest of all, the National Education Association.

The Federation added a transportation department to represent the interests of what had become a major slice of the activities within its jurisdiction. An Asian-American Institute was also added to widen its geographical coverage, as was an Organizing Institute to develop "the science of organizing" in order to "prepare a new generation of organizers through better recruitment, training and placement, as well as by developing both theoretical study and practical application of organizer's skills." Among the materials produced were statistical and tactical data, a "blitz" manual for running fast-paced campaigns, and a labor law handbook.

A delicate policy issue arose at the 1989 convention in the form of a resolution on abortion. The resolutions committee recommended that it be referred to the Executive Council "because the reproductive choice has ethical, religious, civil rights and civil liberty, political, health and economic implications that merit careful and deliberate consideration by the American labor movement." Joyce Miller of the Clothing Workers, the first woman to be elected an AFL-CIO vice-president, urged that the Federation develop a policy without delay, and a delegate of the State County union, a majority of whose members were women, wanted immediate action by the convention. The resolution was referred back.[3] The issue was sidestepped once more at the next convention in 1991 when the Federation deferred to the individual judgment of its members. The proceedings of the 1991 convention stated, "Union members have made it clear that on reproductive issues they believe firmly in their right to act in accordance with their personal convictions."[4] On a related question, the 1989 convention adopted a resolution to the effect that "the AFL-CIO protests any personal actions taken against any worker on the basis of sexual orientation."[5]

The growing number of so-called "contingent" workers provided a new challenge. Included were temporaries, short-time hires, part-timers, and people on call. It was estimated that 60 percent of the temporaries were clerical, 19.5 percent technical, 11.5 percent medical, and 9 percent industrial workers. Women and minorities were over-represented, many of them single mothers who received no employment benefits. To protect regular jobs, unions were urged "to negotiate contract language which will provide that the rights of bargaining unit members shall be protected before any work is relegated to contingent workers."[6] This was a variant of the perennial contracting out problem.

The AFL-CIO was a long-time advocate of a national health system. With reform in the air, discussion became more pointed on the eve of the 1992 election. John Sweeney of the Service Employees told the 1991 convention that "the system of employment-based health coverage we built after the country rejected Harry Truman's proposal is crumbling and crumbling rapidly under relentless health cost inflation." The convention adopted a resolution calling for a unified national health system with a single payer, and urged that the Medicare age be reduced to 60 years.[7]

At the end of the 1980s an upbeat evaluation of union progress during the decade appeared in the *AFL-CIO News*. It averred that despite a hostile NLRB and a less than neutral Supreme Court, there were significant gains in organizing and bargaining. The Clothing and Textile Union had won a contract with J. P. Stevens after a seventeen-year struggle. Beverly Enterprises and the Kingsport Press had finally agreed to bargain. Harvard University had recognized the American Federation of State, County and Municipal Employees (AFSCME) as the representative of 3,500 employees. Some Southern campaigns had been successful.

The ESOP movement had grown, adopted by more than 8,000 firms. The emergence of two-tiered contracts, by which newly hired employees were paid lower wages, was acknowledged to be a negative development, but many were eventually discontinued. Solidarity on the picket line led to union victory where strikes were essential to the preservation of bargaining rights. A Machinists strike of seven weeks against Boeing resulted in a favorable three-year contract. AT&T was induced to sign an agreement including wage increases as well as improved benefits. The article began, "Labor is in good shape after weathering a stormy decade."[8]

Two years later, the same paper published a less favorable evaluation of the social and economic background of the decade entitled "Years of Devastation." Bush's economic record was termed the worst since World War II, with the Gross National Product (GNP) rising less than under any other president since 1942. Wages were stagnant, but managerial executives tripled their pay. Trade deficits made massive inroads into manufacturing jobs, and the North American Free Trade Agreement (NAFTA) threatened to accentuate the trend. The cost of health expenditures soared but forty million people were without insurance. Job safety had deteriorated and legislative remedies had been blocked. Education, family values, and civil rights had suffered. It concluded that the Reagan-Bush legacy was borne on the backs of working people.[9] The unions made it clear that the defeat of Bush in his bid for reelection was essential to improving the causes that they backed. For the first time in many years virtually all the unions, including the Teamsters, backed the Democratic candidate.

NOTES

1. AFL-CIO, *Proceedings of the Nineteenth Constitutional Convention*, 1991, pp. 77–93.

2. *AFL-CIO News*, February 3, 1992.

3. AFL-CIO, *Proceedings of the Eighteenth Constitutional Convention*, 1989, pp. 391 ff.

4. AFL-CIO, *Proceedings of the Nineteenth Constitutional Convention*, 1991, p. 468.

5. AFL-CIO, *Proceedings of the Eighteenth Constitutional Convention*, 1989, p. 347.

6. Ibid., p. 430.

7. AFL-CIO, *Proceedings of the Nineteenth Constitutional Convention*, 1991, pp. 104–123.

8. *AFL-CIO News*, January 8, 1990.

9. *AFL-CIO News*, August 31, 1992.

CHAPTER 9

The First Clinton Years

Labor was euphoric over the victory of Bill Clinton. Lane Kirkland declared to the 1993 AFL-CIO convention that:

we have every right to be proud of the AFL-CIO's role in the 1992 presidential elections, which ended a twelve-year occupation of the White House by Republican, anti-labor forces. Bill Clinton won the election because he understands the plight of working families and promised action on the issues of greatest concern to them. As a result, working Americans now have good reason to expect that government will be back on their side, where it rightfully belongs, working with them in the awesome task of rebuilding our industries, our standard of living and our ideals.[1]

In an address to the convention, Clinton replied: "I became president in part because I wanted a new partnership for the labor movement of America. . . . We are replacing a government that for years worked labor over with a government that works with labor."[2]

Anticipating a New Deal for labor, Kirkland outlined four pieces of legislation that were of the "utmost priority": the Workplace Fairness Act, health care for all, the defeat of NAFTA, and reform of the occupational health and safety laws. The first payoff came quickly. The Family and Medical Leave Act, although not one of the priority items, had been supported by the AFL-CIO and vetoed by President George Bush. Its enactment provided for twelve weeks of unpaid but protected leave for the birth or adoption of a child or serious illness of a spouse, child, parent, or the employee concerned.

After that came a series of disappointments. The NAFTA debacle and the General Agreement on Tariffs and Trade (GATT) treaty, in which foreign trade were the issues, are discussed in Chapter 15. Another trade issue on which the

AFL-CIO had taken a stand also turned out badly. The Federation was a staunch advocate of denying continuation of most-favored-nation status to China until it agreed to improve its record on human rights. The Clinton administration declined to abrogate that status.

A more serious matter was the fate of Workplace Fairness legislation, which was at the top of the priority list. The House passed an appropriate bill by a substantial margin, but when it was under consideration by the Senate, although Clinton had supported it, "it never inspired the midnight phone calls and political arm twisting the White House had lavished on other difficult political issues like the North American Free Trade Agreement or last year's budget."[3] In the end there were only 53 of the 60 Senate votes necessary to invoke cloture and the bill was a dead letter.

A more productive sequel for labor came less than a year later when Clinton attempted to circumvent Congress by issuing an executive order barring the use of permanent replacements for strikers by government contractors. Under the terms of the order, the Secretary of Labor was directed to notify federal agencies whenever a company with a federal contract refused to rehire strikers and insisted instead on retaining the replacements. The contract would then be terminated and future contracts denied to the offender. Lane Kirkland was invited to the White House to witness the signing of the order.

This was not the equivalent of the failed legislation. It did not apply to contracts of less than $100,000, which meant that it would affect only about 10 percent of federal contracts. However, about 90 percent of total contract expenditures goes to companies that would be covered by the order. The President's action was denounced by the Chamber of Commerce as "a gross abuse of power," while Kirkland termed it "a step toward justice in the workplace." There are difficult legal questions involved that the courts will be called upon to adjudicate, but whatever the final outcome, it was an ingenious step toward satisfying the demands of the labor movement and augmenting its economic power.

Universal health care, another item on the AFL-CIO priority list, faded away in the face of Democratic disagreements and Republican onslaughts. Many unions had foregone wage increases in order to gain health protection for their members. Nor was there any improvement in the laws regulating occupational safety and health. Thus the unions were unable to get very far with their legislative agenda during the first two years of the Clinton administration.

WORKER PARTICIPATION

The participation of working people in making business decisions, a practice that is institutionalized as codetermination in Germany and the Scandinavian countries, has not appealed to American unions in the past. Their concern was that the primary loyalty of employees might shift from the union to the enterprise, thus weakening the former. They have argued that this arrangement might work where unions are accepted by employers as permanent and useful social organizations, but not where animosity between labor and management persists and where employers might look to some version of codetermination as a means of crippling unions.

Recent developments have forced the unions to take another look at the issue; those that occurred in the steel and automobile industries are detailed in Chapter 16. The movement has gone farthest in the airlines, where unions have gained considerable influence in operational decisions.

In October 1990, the board of directors of United Airlines rejected a union offer to buy the company. Four years later, the Pilots union agreed, in return for 55 percent of the company stock, to accept a pay cut of almost 16 percent, and the Machinists of 10 percent. The unions were to name three members of the board of directors, and pledged that there would be no strikes for six years. This has given them control of the airline, a fact that has been emphasized in company advertising.

Then there was the case of Northwest Airlines in 1993. The unions received 30 percent of the company's preferred stock with the privilege of converting it to common stock, as well as three seats on the board. The pilots agreed to a wage reduction of $365 million over a three-year period, and the other unions made contributions in wages and changes in working rules. Similar concessions enabled the unions to acquire a 45 percent stake as part of a Trans World Airlines bankruptcy settlement. US Air has been moving in the same direction. This leaves only American and Delta, of the major American airlines, outside the union participatory network.

The Executive Council of the AFL-CIO set up a committee consisting of union presidents and department heads to develop a consistent policy for these arrangements. Its report was published in February 1994, under the title "The New American Workplace: A Labor Perspective." It is an important document in that it comes to grips with an issue that is of concern to working people in many countries.

The present system, the report states, is no longer appropriate. "The time has come for labor and management to surmount past enmities and forge the kind of partnership which can generate more productive, democratic and humane systems of work." The planning and making of decisions are currently the function of an elite group of managerial and expert personnel with little worker contribution. Wages and working conditions are driven down in the search for profits, and workers are denied job satisfaction. Unions have been able to carve out certain areas of control through collective bargaining, but management retains all residual rights.

A new model of work organization should be based on five principles:

1. The traditional dichotomy between thinking and doing, conception and execution, should be rejected. This would require a redistribution of some authority to make decisions from management to teams of workers.

2. Jobs should be designed to include a greater variety of skills and tasks and workers should have greater responsibility for output.

3. Management structure should be flatter in place of the vertical hierarchical model, which tends to be authoritarian.

4. Workers, through their trade unions, should have a decision-making role at all levels of the enterprise, not only the workplace.

5. The rewards realized from management restructuring should be distributed equitably through labor-management negotiations. This could take the form of higher wages, profit-sharing, stock ownership, or the like.

The report stresses the necessity of worker representation by free and independent unions. Employers would have to recognize the legitimacy of unions and end all efforts to eradicate them. Changes in work organization would be determined by collective bargaining. Unions and management would have equal roles in developing and implementing new work systems. There would continue to be conflicting interests, however, particularly with respect to the division of the economic pie. The report states, "A labor organization that fails to recognize the divergent interests of workers and employers is not worthy of the name."

Up to the present time, the report continues, changes in work have been rare because management is reluctant to yield any control and union leaders have tended to rally workers against management initiatives. The report asserts:

The overwhelming majority of workplaces are still operated along traditional lines and likely will continue that way for a very long time . . . resistance to change is embedded in the culture of virtually every workplace. The national interest requires the building of strong enterprises not governed on the basis of short-run concerns.

The AFL-CIO concedes that it has been "insufficiently attentive to the needs of trade union leaders who are on the firing lines." They should have more information and assistance in responding to management proposals and formulating their own. The Federation should help by sponsoring conferences and seminars for its affiliates. The document makes it abundantly clear that the basic requisite for union support of a new work model is untrammeled worker rights to choose their collective representatives. Once this has been done, employers must respect their choice. It is the union, on behalf of the individual worker, that participates in determining strategic business policies.

Codetermination was imposed upon employers in Germany and Scandinavia by legislation, even though employers in those countries were more favorably disposed toward unions than is generally true in the United States. There is an occasional American enterprise that is prepared to go this route without legislation. For example, Levi Strauss, the largest apparel manufacturer in the United States, agreed to recognize the Amalgamated Clothing Workers as representative of its employees on the basis of card signatures, in return for union assistance in raising productivity in manufacturing and shipment of goods. One of the results of the agreement was a sharp increase in union membership.[4]

There has been no rush to emulate Levi Strauss. A more typical event for the Clothing Workers was a campaign to organize the Tultex Corporation, a manufacturer of fleece for sports apparel, located in Martinsville, Virginia. The union had been trying without success to organize the company for years. It lost an election in 1990, but won by a substantial majority in 1994 after employee compensation had been reduced. It was the biggest Southern victory for the Amalgamated since it signed with J. P. Stevens in North Carolina twenty years earlier.[5]

INTERNAL AFFAIRS

The Amalgamated Clothing Workers agreed to a merger with the Ladies' Garment Workers Union, creating a 350,000-member union named the Union of Needletrades, Industrial and Textile Employees, ending one of the longest feuds in the history of American labor.

The Coalition of Black Trade Unionists, a successor to an organization founded by A. Philip Randolph, held its twentieth anniversary meeting in Chicago in 1991. Unlike the earlier group, it was firmly allied with the labor movement. Its president was William Lucy, secretary-treasurer of the State County union, the most important position held by a black in the AFL-CIO. The coalition had twenty-seven chapters representing seventy-seven national unions; its purpose was to help promote organization among blacks.

The Executive Council tried still another tack to induce unions to affiliate with state and local central bodies. A target of 40 percent membership affiliation was set for each union; if the union failed to achieve it, a penalty of one cent per month would be added to its per capita payment to the AFL-CIO. The target would be raised by 2 percent a year until 1997, when it would reach 50 percent The funds collected in this manner will be used to subsidize the central bodies.

THE COMMISSION ON THE FUTURE OF WORKER-MANAGEMENT RELATIONS

This commission was appointed by President Clinton on March 24, 1993, to study and report on three questions:

1. What new methods or institutions would raise productivity through labor-management cooperation and employee participation?

2. What changes should be made in the law and practice of collective bargaining to do the above plus reduce conflict and delay?

3. What should be done to increase the resolution of workplace problems by the parties themselves without recourse to courts and the government?

The AFL-CIO looked upon the commission as a promising instrument that the administration might employ to help secure some of the objectives frustrated by congressional inaction. As Kirkland remarked, "We expect that a fair hearing by this commission will produce but one conclusion—that the law, as it stands, is not sufficient to ensure working people their basic right to a trade union."[6] The commission consisted primarily of academics, with one member each from labor and management.

After a great deal of research and a number of hearings, the commission delivered its report in December 1994. It covered a wide range of subjects, including a number of programs administered by the Labor Department. The discussion here is limited to the areas of greatest concern to the labor movement.

1. The commission recommended that the National Labor Relations Act be clarified "to insure nonunion employee participation programs are not found to be unlawful simply because they involve discussions of 'terms and conditions' of work or compensation as long as such discussion is incidental to the broad purposes of these programs. At the same time, the Commission reaffirms that these programs are not a substitute for independent unions. The law should continue to make it illegal to set up or operate company-dominated forms of employee representation."[7]

A survey conducted for the commission revealed that two-thirds of employees at enterprises without some form of worker involvement programs favored the discussions referred to in the report. The commission emphasized that such arrangements, which were more frequent in union than in nonunion plants, were to complement rather than replace union representation. It also pointed out that many professionals and other employees were barred from such discussions because their duties involved a modicum of supervision, and suggested that the definitions in the law be changed to give these people the right to engage in collective bargaining if they wished to do so.

2. The second major recommendation would mandate representation elections before rather than after hearings on legal issues, and within two weeks of an NLRB determination that a sufficient number of workers had expressed a desire to be represented by a union. The commission had determined that on the average, seven months elapsed between the filing of a petition for an election and the conduct of the election. This was in answer to the union complaint that the delay gave employers time to wage antiunion campaigns.

3. Another union complaint was that activists were often victimized during organizing campaigns, and that a long period of time usually elapsed before the employer was obliged to make restitution, thus impairing the campaigns. The commission recommended that injunctions be used "to remedy discriminatory actions against employees that occur in organizing campaigns and first contract negotiations."[8] Employers and unions should be urged to use card checks rather than elections to determine whether a union represented a majority.

4. Some employers engage in the tactic of lengthy delays in reaching agreements with unions that have won elections for the first time. The commission

recommended that in such cases, negotiations be assisted by mediation, and that a First Contract Advisory Board be established and empowered "to use a wide range of options to resolve disputes, including referring them back to the parties to negotiate with the right to strike or lockout, further mediation or fact finding, or use of arbitration in a form best suited to the circumstances of the particular case."[9] This includes the possibility of compulsory arbitration, a drastic step well beyond customary practice in the private sector.

Among the other recommendations was one urging Congress to reverse a Supreme Court decision limiting union access to privately owned but publicly used spaces[10]; and changes in the treatment of contingent workers and in affirmative action. Suffice it to say that there is little if anything in the forty pages of the report in which this latter group of recommendations is discussed with which unions would disagree.

Shortly after the report was issued, the *AFL-CIO News* ran a brief summary of its contents and expressed disappointment with the results. The reason for this negative reaction may be found in the only dissent in the document, that by Douglas A. Fraser, former president of the UAW and the labor representative on the commission. His objection was to the very first recommendation, that having to do with employee participation in nonunion situations: "Because I an deeply committed to the principle of workplace democracy, I cannot join in any statement that proclaims that you can have fully effective worker-management cooperation without having a truly equal partnership based upon workers having an independent voice."[11] A reading of *The New American Workplace* should have made it clear that the existence of a union was a *sine qua non* for the willingness of the AFL-CIO to endorse any form of partnership between labor and management.

The report did recommend many changes in the interpretation and administration of labor legislation that the unions strongly desired. It is possible that they could have been persuaded to accept the report with some enthusiasm if there had been some prospect of congressional ratification of key recommendations. But the timing was bad. Between the preparation of the report and its promulgation the Republican Party had attained a congressional majority, leaving little likelihood that the bulk of the report would be enacted into law. The portion of the report to which Fraser objected stuck out like a sore thumb, and there was obviously no desire on the part of the unions to encourage any move in the direction of nonunion partnerships.

The fruits of the Clinton victory in 1992 fell short of union expectations. The NAFTA and GATT treaties, which they had opposed strenuously, were ratified by the U.S. government. Workplace fairness legislation and a national health scheme failed to be enacted. Hopes for labor law reform were dashed when the Republicans gained control of Congress in 1994.

Not all has been negative during Clinton's first term. The Secretary of Labor, Robert B. Reich, was as pro-union as anyone who had held that position before him. There was no talk of using the Department to nullify the Davis-Bacon Act or any other regulation of significance to the labor movement. On the contrary, labor had a friend in the White House, in sharp contrast to the Reagan-Bush eras, best exemplified by the executive order on permanent replacement of strikers. But what stood in the way of greater hope for the future, midway in the Clinton tenure, were two years of Robert Dole–Newt Gingrich domination of Congress and the bleak prospect of a Republican victory in the 1996 presidential election. Thomas Donohue expressed it well at a meeting of the Executive Council in February 1995 when he said, "We had hoped to change the labor laws to make it easier for people at work. That hope is gone now, and we have to say, 'My God, we have to do more ourselves.' This is the shifting of gears that took place here this week."[12]

NOTES

1. AFL-CIO, *President's Report to the Twentieth Constitutional Convention*, 1993, p. 1.
2. AFL-CIO, *Proceedings of the Twentieth Constitutional Convention*, 1993, p. 1.
3. *New York Times*, July 13, 1994, p. D18.
4. *New York Times*, October 13, 1994, p. D6.
5. *New York Times*, September 11, 1994, p. 21.
6. AFL-CIO, *Report of the Executive Council to the Twentieth Constitutional Convention*, 1993, p. 5.
7. Commission on the Future of Worker-Management Relations, *Report and Recommendations* (Washington, DC: Government Printing Office, December 1994), p. xvii.
8. Ibid., p. 18.
9. Ibid., p. 22.
10. See Chapter 13.
11. *Report and Recommendations*, p. 14.
12. *New York Times*, February 26, 1995, p. 23.

CHAPTER 10

Union Organizing and the Employer Counteroffensive

The years since the merger have been marked by the most sustained employer campaign against trade unionism in American labor history. There were earlier episodes, but they were neither as professionally managed nor as effective in the long run. The decline of the labor movement in the last two decades cannot be attributed solely to employer opposition, but it certainly played a significant role. For their part, the unions tried to adapt their organizational tactics and strategy to the new political and economic environment, with only limited success.

Two indices may be cited to show the rise in employer efforts to frustrate the unionization of their employees: the number of unfair labor practice charges filed by unions with the NLRB and the results of representation elections conducted by the Board. An upward trend in the first would suggest an increase in allegedly illegal employer activities, and a decline in union election victories would indicate how successful these activities have been.

The data related to these indices appear in Table 10.1. Total AFL-CIO membership rose by only 10 percent from 1955 to 1990, so that it would be difficult to attribute the huge increase in unfair labor practice charges to larger cohorts of complaining workers. The number of elections held was almost identical in 1955 and 1990, though there had been a sharp rise in the 1970s. The most striking aspect of the election data is the large decline in the number of elections won by unions between these two years. Several studies have concluded that the series are linked; that union losses are the consequence of illegal employer conduct.[1]

Table 10.1
National Labor Relations Board Cases, 1955–1990

Year	Unfair labor[a] practice cases received	Number of[b] elections held	Employees eligible to vote	Percent of elections won by unions
1955	6,171	4,215	515,995	67.6
1960	11,357	6,380	483,964	58.6
1965	15,800	7,776	544,536	60.2
1970	21,038	8,074	608,558	55.2
1975	31,253	8,577	568,920	48.2
1980	44,063	8,198	521,602	45.7
1985	32,685	4,614	254,220	42.4
1990	33,833	4,210	261,385	46.7

[a]Includes a small number of cases filed by employers.
[b]Includes elections involving more than one union.
Source: Annual Reports of the National Labor Relations Board.

ORGANIZING CAMPAIGNS

The leadership of the AFL-CIO was aware of the need to press organization, as evidenced by such institutional innovations as the Department of Organization, the Organizing Institute, and the strategic approaches committee. But the energy and financial resources had to come from individual unions. A study of organizing expenditures by 27 unions, representing half of all union members, for the period 1953 to 1977 found that there had been a significant increase, although they declined slightly as a percentage of total expenditures. There was a more significant decline when measured against the potential pool of unorganized workers.[2]

Comparable data for subsequent years are not available, but an analysis of NLRB election returns to gauge the extent of organizational efforts was published in 1990. The conclusions:

There was no widespread recovery from the sharp drop in organizing activity that occurred from 1981 to 1982, and in most cases the decline continued. . . . the only notable exceptions to the trend were the cases of the Operating Engineers and Steelworkers and the construction industry. . . . the decline in union organizing is severe. . . . although the certification election process may not have run completely dry for unions, it has certainly come very close in doing so in the years since the recent recession.[3]

The authors recognize the possibility that more unions have been bypassing the NLRB mechanisms and dealing directly with employers, but they doubt that this would alter their general conclusions.

Joseph Beirne, president of the Communications Workers, wrote in 1965 that his union was facing a completely new labor force as a result of technological change. A few years earlier two-thirds of his members were telephone operators; now it was down to less than half and dropping fast. He warned that the slogans of the 1930s were no longer appropriate:

The typical unorganized worker of today does not hate his boss or his company. His place of employment is not a dungeon or a hell hole. His wages may not be all they should be, but they are a long way from starvation. More than the assembly line worker, the white collar worker and the technicians do take a certain pride in their skills, a pride not unlike that of the craftsman.[4]

The new workers were often reluctant to accept the loss of employment involved in a strike.

When William Kircher was head of the AFL-CIO Department of Organization in the late 1960s he commissioned a poll in California to determine the attitudes of potential members toward unions. What emerged was that young people voted for unions only 4 percent less than the average; that women tended to be more receptive to unionism than men; that conservatives were more inclined than liberals to vote against unions. Two-thirds of those who had voted against Reagan for governor favored unions. Married workers were slightly more pro-union than single workers. And to the question, "What do you think influenced you or your co-workers most in a union campaign?" face-to-face contact with organizers and fellow employees ranked highest, followed by leaflets and home visits. The employers' best weapons against unions were speeches to a captive audience and talks by supervisors and foremen to small groups of employees.[5]

A more recent survey of ninety-seven union organizers representing fifteen unions provided more detail about the manner in which they approached their jobs. Small groups and the distribution of union literature were the most common approaches, while associate status for employees and the development of nonunion associations as a prelude to unionization were the least favored. The issues most frequently stressed were access to grievance machinery, job security, improved benefits, and higher pay. For women, job security and grievance access were less effective than technical training and satisfying work. House visits increased in effectiveness as the proportion of white-collar workers rose. However, the authors of the survey concluded that in general, "there does not seem to be much change in either organizing tactics or issues."[6]

That there had been no change would be disputed by the unions. The corporate campaign, in which pressure is exerted on the finances of the employer, is relatively new. But how effective have such campaigns been? A study of twenty-five actions that were considered to be in this category by the unions involved showed mixed results. Ten were initiated to complement regular organizational drives; nine were started after strikes or lockouts had begun; and the rest were initiated prior to a strike. Those that accompanied traditional organizing drives were likely to yield gains, those complementing strikes had the largest number of failures, and corporate campaigns as a substitute for strikes had only limited success. It was difficult to pinpoint the tactics that worked best. A great deal depended on the nature of the firm and its economic circumstances.[7]

THE FEMALE FACTOR

The transformation of the American labor force that resulted from the large-scale entrance of women has been reflected in the trade unions. The female labor force participation rate rose from 37.7 percent in 1960 to 57.9 percent in 1993. The number of organized women increased from 3.2 million in 1956 to 6.5 million in 1993, and by the latter year almost 40 percent of all union members were women, up from 19 percent in 1956.

Women employees are still less well-organized than men; the relative percentages being 13 to 18.4 percent. But this does not say much about present organizational trends. The two most rapidly growing sectors of the economy, government and services, are where most new female entrants into the labor market have been going. The three most rapidly growing unions in the AFL-CIO, Food and Commercial, State County, and Service, were respectively 51, 50, and 45 percent female in 1990. The decline in the union density ratio has been much smaller for women than for men.

There is a traditional belief that women are more difficult to organize than men, despite early unionization of some occupations that were largely female—clothing workers and telephone operators, for example. This has been attributed to a number of factors: looser female attachment to the labor market, greater concern with domestic responsibilities than with jobs, less time for participation in union activities, and fear of strikes and picket line violence, among other things.

Recent studies and experience have altered this view. Data from a 1984 poll commissioned by the AFL-CIO suggest that the lower female unionization rate is due to the fact that women have had less opportunity to become acquainted with unions and to vote for them. Given the same opportunity, as many women as men vote pro-union. In white-collar occupations, and even in blue-collar trades, there is a trend in this direction. In short, when women are confronted with the same decision to make as their male counterparts under similar circumstances, they are at least as likely as men to vote Union Yes.[8]

Another question is whether the growing feminization of the labor movement owes anything to new techniques of organization. The results of Marion Crain's recent study—based upon interviews, questionnaires, and correspondence with directors of organization and field personnel of a number of unions—throw a good deal of light on the efforts unions are making to attract women members. Special reference is made to the Service Employees International Union (SEIU), the most rapidly growing organization in the AFL-CIO.

1. Of eight organization directors interviewed, seven said that women were more receptive to unions than men, one found the two equal. Almost all female field organizers believed that women were easier to organize, or no more difficult (including the SEIU organizers), and a majority of the men agreed with them.

2. Some organizers felt that women had less experience with unions and had picked up fewer negative preconceptions about them. A special effort had to be made to tell them about union benefits, but once they had committed themselves, women were unshakeable. It was also suggested that women had more pent-up anger in the way they were treated on the job, making them more militant.

3. The secondary wage earner status of many women was looked upon as a favorable factor. They were more willing to engage in strikes and risk income because the family had a primary wage earner.

4. All but two of the directors believed that gender was irrelevant to organizing strategy or style. The field personnel were more ambivalent. Eighty-five percent of them disagreed with the following statement: ''Organizing strategies that are successful with one group of workers will be successful with all groups of workers.'' Half the field personnel believed that a different and sometimes unconventional style was more effective with women. Female organizers in particular found it useful to emphasize issues of more concern to women—work conflicts and workplace discrimination, for example.

5. More women organizers have been hired in recent years. This is difficult to do, since organizers are poorly paid, have the toughest jobs, and have a high burn-out rate. Women are also reluctant to commit themselves to irregular hours and a good deal of traveling.

6. Some organizational directors, particularly in manufacturing, were critical of their unions for unwillingness to commit sufficient funds for them to operate successfully. Figures of 2 to 4 percent of budgeted costs were cited as the norm. The unions seemed to believe that money was better spent for servicing the current membership. Those that had done best had created special entities to organize particular groups; the SEIU and the UAW were cited in this respect.

7. Apart from the SEIU, the organizational directors observed that that there was little targeting of specific enterprises. The initiative generally came from disgruntled employees.

8. There was a division of opinion on the value of issues that were primarily of interest to women—day care, comparable worth, sexual harassment, maternity leave. The term ''family issues'' was preferred to ''women's issues.'' Despite some negative views, gender-specific strategies were being pursued, however they were identified.

9. Finally, the SEIU appears to have departed more than most unions from customary organizing attitudes and techniques, focusing on participation in workplace decision-making and other strategies that women seemed to favor.[9]

The strategic approaches committee and the Organizing Institute were institutional devices that the AFL-CIO created to promote targeting and a more scientific approach to organization. A committee on the needs of the working family was another response to the growing importance of the female factor.

Table 10.2
Female Membership and Leadership in Selected Large Unions, 1990

Organization	Percent of women members	Percent of women officers or board members
Food and Commercial Workers	51	8
State, County, and Municipal Workers	50	17
Service Employees	45	34
Teachers	65	32
Communications Workers	52	6
Clothing and Textile Workers	61	20
Ladies' Garment Workers	83	22
Hotel and Restaurant Employees	48	4
National Education Association (Ind.)	60	67

Source: Ruth Millman, ''The New Gender Politics in Organized Labor,'' Industrial Relations Research Association, Fortieth Annual Proceedings, p. 351.

Convention resolutions have called for federal support for day care. But the AFL-CIO has tended to steer clear of such controversial issues as abortion and the achievment of pay equity through job evaluation. As far as union leadership is concerned, there is still a large female deficit, as the data in Table 10.2 indicate. The American labor movement remains male-dominated.

THE EMPLOYER OFFENSIVE

A good way to introduce this subject is through a famous case of prolonged employer resistance to unionization. This was the struggle between the Textile Workers Union and J. P. Stevens & Company, the second largest textile manufacturer in the United States, employing about 45,000 workers mainly in North and South Carolina. Stevens produces a diversity of products but generally does not market under its own name.

The union initiated an organizing campaign against a Stevens plant in 1963. The company responded by discharging eighteen workers who were ordered reinstated by an NLRB trial examiner. This order was sustained by the NLRB and by the U.S. Supreme Court after going through the lower courts. The reinstated workers were awarded back pay of $194,000. The company was not discouraged. In 1967, it was ordered to reinstate eighteen workers at six different plants plus four additional workers in 1968, all with back pay.

Two years later, the NLRB directed Stevens to bargain with the union in one of its plants and once again to reinstate discharged workers. The Circuit Court of Appeals upheld this decision and the Supreme Court declined to hear the case. Finally in 1969, the NLRB filed a contempt charge against the company for continuing to flout its orders. It took three years for the Circuit Court to hold the company in contempt; it was obliged to reinstate ten employees and pay them $106,000.

In 1970, Stevens cut the wages of employees at its Statesboro plant immediately after the NLRB had ordered it to bargain with the union, and was eventually fined $72,000. At the same time, the company was charged with the illegal discharge of seven workers at a Georgia plant and their reinstatement was ordered. A few days before the opening of a trial for contempt, it was discovered that listening devices had been planted in the rooms of several discharged employees who were participating in an organizing campaign. Faced with an indictment of the offending officials, Stevens settled for $50,000.

In 1974, after a majority of its employees at a Roanoke plant had voted for the union, Stevens agreed to bargain, but it refused to discuss wages, seniority, or grievance arbitration, and the negotiations dragged on. A federal court in 1977 ordered Stevens to give the unions access to all its sixty-three plants in North and South Carolina and to educate its supervisors on the subject of union rights. A national consumer boycott of its products was initiated.

An AFL-CIO corporate campaign led to the resignation of the Stevens board chairman from the boards of directors of the Manufacturers Hanover Bank and the New York Life Insurance Company, which had been financing the company. Several members of Stevens own board resigned. The union won a number of elections in various plants in 1980. Six Catholic bishops located in the South endorsed the union campaign, there were more reinstatement orders, and the courts found that the company had not been bargaining in good faith. The Metropolitan Life Insurance Company, which held 40 percent of the company's long-term debt, was faced by a challenge to its continued relationship with Stevens at a stockholders' meeting.

An agreement was finally reached in October 1980, seventeen years after the union had begun to organize, which provided grievance arbitration and wage adjustments. The union had successfully prosecuted a hundred NLRB complaints over the period of conflict.[10] It took three additional years before industrial relations at Stevens took on a degree of normalcy. The union then dropped all outstanding complaints against Stevens in return for a million dollar payment, and proceeded to organize employees who were not yet under contract.

There are other examples of employer resistance, though the tenacity of the Stevens' management was unique. The Kohler Company of Wisconsin and the Kingsport Press in Tennessee suffered lengthy strikes and court proceedings before they finally capitulated. In the case of the latter, it required twenty-five years and a change of ownership before labor peace was achieved. More recently, the Caterpillar Company has entered the same employer league.

A number of more subtle tactics were devised than those crude ones used by Stevens. Among them were pre-employment screening to exclude individuals whose ethnic backgrounds might dispose them to favor unions; sending antiunion letters to family members; the use of bulletin boards as well as radio, television, and newspaper ads; meeting workers in small groups; spreading fear of job loss through rumors of plant closings; transfer of work to other locations; and harsh disciplinary measures.

Many employers have resorted to a burgeoning profession to help them plan their opposition campaigns—antiunion consultants. These people are mainly psychologists and specialists in labor law who can advise them on the legality and effectiveness of their tactics. They provide training courses and manuals for supervisors, traveling seminars, material for speeches and bulletin boards, attitude surveys, and espionage techniques. Employers are often advised never to agree to a consent election but rather to delay; never to reach agreement on the appropriate bargaining unit—anything to deflect an organizing campaign. A union has an advantage in that it can time its petition for representation until it estimates that it has a majority, but the employer can seek to nullify this advantage by raising legal objections.

Specialist consultants were not unknown in the past, but what makes them of particular current interest is their widespread extent. A survey conducted by the AFL-CIO in 1983 found that outside consultants or lawyers directed counter-organizing drives in about three-quarters of the union campaigns. Advice tended to continue after a union had won an election, and in one-third of those cases the employer refused to negotiate an agreement. Federation officials have identified 400 firms employing over 6,000 experts engaged in this occupation.[11]

Another indicator of the unwillingness of many employers to engage in collective bargaining on a long-term basis is decertification. Under certain circumstances specified by law, employees in a bargaining unit represented by a union can petition the NLRB for an election to revoke the representation status of the union. There has been a steady increase in the number of such elections and a decline in the ability of incumbent unions to hold their members. Employers have argued that these trends represent growing discontent with unionism, but the more likely explanation is that employers have encouraged decertification petitions using the same tactics as in obstructing organization.

STRIKES

The strike or lockout is the ultimate weapon open to the parties when collective bargaining fails to resolve a labor dispute. The data in Table 10.3 reveal a remarkable decline in work stoppages (the great majority are strikes) from 1960 to 1993, and in their severity as measured by the consequent number of days idle as a percentage of working time. The figures for a particular year are influenced by special circumstances; for example, the heavy loss of working time in 1970 reflects major strikes in the automobile and rubber tire industries.

The sharp decline in strikes after 1980 is particularly notable. It is probable that an important factor in this development was the increased threat and use of striker replacements. What makes this such a devastating weapon is that a de-

Table 10.3
Work Stoppages in the United States, 1960–1993

Year	Number	Days idle as a percentage of working time
1960	222	0.09
1965	268	0.10
1970	381	0.29
1975	235	0.09
1980	187	0.09
1985	54	0.03
1990	44	0.02
1993	35	0.01

Source: Statistical Abstract of the United States, 1994, p. 438.

termined employer can rid itself of a union at an optimal time without running afoul of the law. A wage or other concession can be demanded at the expiration of a contract that the union cannot accept and still retain its hold on the employees, and thus the employer can deliberately provoke a strike after a sufficiently long period of negotiating without being held in violation of the law. This is a particularly effective strategy during a recession when unemployment is running high.

A decade ago a comprehensive study of industrial relations, in commenting on an earlier theory that the strike was fading away as a union tactic, concluded that "While there is some downward trend in strike-time lost, the notion that strikes are now diminishing is now recognized to be inaccurate. Strikes remain part of labor-management relations."[12] It now appears that 1980 was a downward turning point in the use of the strike weapon, brought about by the successful employer offensive and the growing popularity of the replacement option. The data in Table 10.3 suggest that while the strike has not faded away, its importance in labor relations has certainly diminished. The enactment of legislation to deprive employers of the replacement option does not necessarily guarantee unions greater success in organization and collective bargaining, but it is clear why the AFL-CIO has placed such legislation at the top of its agenda.

NOTES

1. Richard B. Freeman and James L. Medoff, *What Do Unions Do?* (New York: Basic Books, 1984), p. 237; William N. Cooke, "The Rising Toll of Discrimination Against Union Activities," *Industrial Relations* (Fall 1985), p. 437.

2. Paula B. Voos, "Trends in Union Organizing Expenditures, 1953–1977," *Industrial and Labor Relations Review* (October 1984), p. 437.

3. Gary N. Chaison and Dileep G. Dhavala, "A Note on the Severity of the Decline in Union Organizing Activity," *Industrial and Labor Relations Review* (April 1990), pp. 371–372.

4. AFL-CIO, *American Federationist* (January 1965), p. 22.

5. AFL-CIO, *American Federationist* (March 1969), p. 22.

6. Monty L. Lynn and Jozell Brister, "Trends in Union Organizing Issues and Tactics," *Industrial Relations* (Winter 1990), p. 104.

7. Paul Jarley and Cheryl L. Maranto, "Union Corporate Campaigns: An Assessment," *Industrial and Labor Relations Review* (July 1990), p. 505.

8. For example, see Lisa Schur and Douglas L. Cruse, "Gender Differences in Attitudes Toward Unions," *Industrial and Labor Relations Review* (October 1992), p. 89.

9. These summary points are from Marion Crain, "Gender and Union Organizing," *Industrial and Labor Relations Review* (January 1984), pp. 227–248.

10. For a detailed chronology of this strike, see AFL-CIO, "J. P. Stevens, Anatomy of An Outlaw," *American Federationist* (April 1976), p. 1, and *American Federationist* (December 1980), p. 1.

11. AFL-CIO, *Report of the Executive Council to the Fifteenth Constitutional Convention*, 1983, pp. 118–120.

12. Freeman and Medoff, *What Do Unions Do?*, p. 237.

CHAPTER 11

The Public Sector and Professionals

Employees in the public sector and professionals have become important targets for union organizers. Their ranks have swelled while those of manual workers in private employment have thinned. The unions in these sectors have helped slow the decline in union density. Yet there is still a long way to go before they replace the traditional core of union power.

THE PUBLIC SECTOR

There were 7.3 million government employees in the United States in 1956, of whom 915,000, or 12.5 percent were members of AFL-CIO unions or independents. By 1993, government employment had risen to 18.6 million, of whom 7 million, or 38 percent, were organized. The largest subsector in the latter year was education, 44 percent of the total, followed by health and public safety with about 9 percent each. The share of total public employment by major government branch was as follows (1992):

federal	16.3 percent
state	24.5 percent
local	59.2 percent

It is difficult to determine precisely how many public employees are currently members of AFL-CIO unions because many national unions organize in both the public and private sectors. Table 11.1 contains the membership figures for AFL-CIO unions that are primarily in the public sector, but it is not a complete catalog of public sector organization. The largest union in the country, the in-

Table 11.1
Membership of AFL-CIO Unions Primarily in the Public Sector (thousands)

Federal

Postal

National Association of Letter Carriers	210
American Postal Workers Union	249

Civil Service

American Federation of Government Employees	149

State and Local

Civil Service

American Federation of State, County, and Municipal Employees	1,167

Safety

International Association of Fire Fighters	151
International Union of Police Associations	22

Education

American Federation of Teachers	574
American Federation of School Administrators	11

Source: AFL-CIO, *Report of the Executive Council to the Nineteenth Biennial Convention*, 1993, pp. 57–61.

dependent National Education Association, consists mainly of publicly employed teachers.

The Golden Age of public sector unionism was the two decades from 1860 to 1880. There has been subsequent stagnation, and even decline. The American Federation of Government Employees, the principal union representing civil service and wage grade federal workers, peaked at 255,000 members in 1975 and then fell steadily to 140,000 in 1993. Estimates for public sector unions as a whole vary, but for the 1980s there appears to have been stagnation at best.[1]

Federal workers fall into two main groups for collective bargaining. The postal workers are among the most highly organized groups in the country. The American Postal Workers Union was formed by the merger of six smaller unions in 1971 in response to the Postal Reorganization Act of 1970. This legislation placed postal workers under the National Labor Relations Act except for one provision—they were denied the right to strike. However, they can invoke compulsory arbitration in the event of a bargaining impasse, which puts the Postal Workers and a brother union, the National Association of Letter Carriers, in a position to provide strong representation for their members. Data for 1991 suggest that these two unions represented 90 percent of postal employees for bargaining purposes, although only 60 percent were actually members.

Over two million nonpostal employees are governed by the Civil Service

Reform Act of 1976. Unions in this area are handicapped by the fact that they cannot bargain over wages, hours, or other benefits, which are fixed by Congress, though they have the right to prosecute grievances. They cannot negotiate a union or agency shop, with the result that half the employees they represent are not dues-paying members.

Most public employees work for state and local governments, where the picture is more complicated. A number of unions are involved and jurisdictions are tangled. Every state has different laws determining labor relations with its employees, supplemented by city and county regulations. As of 1993, some twenty-three states and the District of Columbia afforded their employees comprehensive collective bargaining rights, covering more than nine million state and local government workers. Thirteen states had bargaining laws for specified occupational groups; of the 2.5 million employees in these states, 750,000 were under these laws. Fourteen states had no bargaining legislation for their four million employees.

Overall, 5.7 million of the 15.5 million state and local employees do not have collective bargaining rights. Almost 60 percent of the employees who have such rights are covered by a union contract, although not all are union members.[2] The bargaining laws are very important to the chances of successful organization. A study of the years 1977 to 1982 concluded that "changes in unionization attributable to duty to bargain laws are so large that they account for nearly all of the differences in average unionization rates between states with and without these laws."[3]

Generally speaking, public employees do not have the right to strike, although there are exceptions. Nevertheless strikes do occur even where they are legally prohibited. The penalties may include fines for the unions involved and imprisonment for their officers, but they are less draconian in states that have strong labor movements. New York has had more than its share of strikes by transport workers, sanitation men, teachers, and other groups, but there has been nothing paralleling the airport controllers' imbroglio. Where collective bargaining is recognized, state and municipal officials tend to be less unyielding than the Federal government.

Public sector unionism appears to have yielded substantial returns to members. This is not only a matter of wages and other benefits but also of the pursuit of grievances and job stability. Employers in the public sector are not constrained by the competitive consequences of higher labor costs. Their problem is to convince state legislatures to appropriate sufficient funds, a political task, which may become more difficult with growing fiscal stringency.[4]

The major union involved in state and local employment is the American Federation of State, County, and Municipal Employees (AFSCME); its main competitor is the Service Employees International Union (SEIU), both of which are discussed below. Among the other unions that have a substantial public sector membership are the Teamsters and the Laborers. The Firefighters Union, an old AFL organization, has achieved a substantial degree of organization in almost all major cities and in many smaller ones as well. The police are not as well organized; their largest union is the independent Fraternal Order of Police.

There were 3.4 million elementary and secondary school teachers in the United States in 1992. The two organizations representing them are the American Federation of Teachers, an affiliate of the AFL-CIO that has a membership of 574,000, and the National Education Association, whose 2.2 million members make it the largest union in the country. There have been many talks between the two regarding a possible merger, but they have come to naught. In any event, teachers are among the best organized occupational groups in the U.S.

Despite the rapid rise of public sector unionism there is still plenty of room for expansion. Whether this will occur depends as much on legislative change as on union activism. There are still twenty-seven states that do not confer full bargaining rights on all their employees. They tend to be the states that have resisted unions in the past, and progress may be slow.

Aside from political obstacles, public sector unions face at least two threats. One is federal grants to the states which may suffer from attempts to reduce the federal deficit. The AFL-CIO has consistently advocated higher grants, but since 1980 they have tended to stagnate in dollars of constant purchasing power. The second threat is from privatization. States and municipalities that are hard pressed to balance their budgets—many of them are bound by constitutional constraints to do so—may seek to reduce the financial pressure by turning government functions over to private firms. The contracting-out of sanitation services has been common, and recently some schools have gone the same way. Needless to say, the public sector unions are strongly opposed to this trend despite the greater ease of bargaining with private contractors. The public purse has greater attraction.

PROFESSIONALS

The Bureau of Labor Statistics estimated that 16.9 million professionals were employed in 1993. According to the AFL-CIO, three million of them were union members in 1990, and including those in independent organizations, this implies a density ratio of about 18 percent. Several points are to be noted: First, more than one-third of all professionals work for the various governments, and 80 percent of professionals who are represented in collective bargaining are in the public sector. Only 10 percent of private sector professionals bargain collectively.[5] Unionization of professionals has thus been largely a function of the rise in public sector organization. Second, professional organization reflects to a considerable extent the growth of the teachers' unions in the public sector.

Some professional groups have long been part of the labor movement. The American Federation of Musicians, formed in 1896, was down to 47,000 members in 1993 from 250,000 in 1955, a victim of technological change. The Newspaper Guild, in which journalists and other news employees are organized, had 21,000 members in both these years. Movie and theater actors have been unionized for many years. The AFL-CIO established a Department for Professional Employees in 1977, and 29 unions are currently affiliated with it.

A brief review of the status of unions that cater to professionals may serve to present a better picture of the degree of attachment by professionals to the labor movement.

Office and Professional Employees International Union. This union was first chartered by the AFL in 1945 for office workers, the term "professional" was added to its title in 1965. At that time it had 59,000 members, most of them clericals, and it managed to recruit 30,000 more by 1993. New York City has been the locus of its most intensive efforts, though it has made little headway in the large banks and brokerage houses. It does represent the employees of the New York Stock Exchange, and has been somewhat more successful in the insurance industry. It was the first union to develop an organizing campaign against Blue Cross/Blue Shield, but it has since faced intense competition from other unions. A study of the union came to the conclusion that the union was underfinanced and tended to concentrate on small targets.[6] Almost seven million people work in the finance, insurance, and real estate industries, which remain largely nonunion. Employer opposition has been a negative factor, particularly in suburban areas in which many firms are located.

Health Professionals. There has been a good deal of organization among nonprofessionals in the expanding health industry, but only the nurses in the professional occupations. Until 1974, nonprofit hospital employees did not enjoy the protection of collective bargaining legislation, but the health care amendments enacted in that year corrected this omission. The independent American Nurses Association (ANA) had almost 200,000 members by the end of the 1980s. AFSCME set up a subsidiary body, the United Nurses of America, that claims a membership of 36,000. As for bargaining representation, about one-fifth of the nation's registered nurses are covered by collective agreements: 133,000 by the ANA, 50,000 by the Service Employees, 38,000 by the AFT, and the rest by local associations.

Poor pay and difficult working conditions would seem to make the nurses a good target for the unions. However, their bargaining power has been reduced by the substitution for them of licensed practical nurses; by the importation of foreign nurses; and by the fact that many work only part time. Moreover, 80 percent are in the private sector where they face hospitals that are often in financial straits. On the positive side was a 1988 NLRB ruling permitting eight separate categories of hospital employees each to form separate bargaining units, thus affording the nurses the opportunity of bargaining for themselves and avoiding ties with other groups. The view of the AFL-CIO is that "the favorable outlook for occupational employment growth, the relatively low wages, and the still-large number of unorganized nurses point to great potential for union organizing in the nursing field."[7]

There have been sporadic efforts to organize physicians, but nothing much has come of them. There were 578,000 practicing physicians in the country in

1992, of whom about half belonged to the American Medical Association, which has been forced by the evolution of the industry to take on quasi-union functions. It has been very active, for example, in the campaign to put a cap on awards in malpractice suits, a major factor in determining the incomes of its members. There is a small organization, the Union of American Physicians and Dentists, which is also primarily a lobbying group.

What happens in this area depends a good deal on the progress of health schemes. If large numbers of doctors become, in effect, employees of large health maintenance organizations, there is a distinct possibility that they will organize, as they have in countries that have national health programs. Poorly paid and hard-working hospital interns and residents might seem to constitute an easier target, and they have organized here and there. They face two difficulties: Their status is temporary, and the NLRB has ruled that they are students rather than employees and therefore do not have the protection of the labor laws.

Engineers. About 1.3 million engineers were working in the civilian economy in 1992, most of them for large enterprises. There are a number of professional associations in which they are enrolled, the largest of which is the Council of Engineers and Scientists. The AFL-CIO has a union that caters to them, the International Federation of Professional and Technical Engineers, with a reported membership of 23,000, mostly in government jobs. Engineers are the largest professional group in the country, apart from the teachers, and are mainly salaried.

There appears to be a generally negative view of trade unions among engineers. Many expect to and do move into management ranks. The large coprporations which employ them help to instill this attitude. They tend to be very status conscious and are reluctant to be associated with nonprofessionals. The outlook for unionization of this profession does not appear to be bright.[8]

Scientists. This large occupational group is split into a number of specialties with varying interests. The only organization that has ventured into labor conditions is the American Chemical Society, which has developed employment guidelines and occasionally monitors management activities. But neither the Chemical Society nor any of the other scientific organizations are engaged in collective bargaining. The fact that a majority of scientists are employed in the public sector or by universities is a divisive factor. Two decades ago an AFL-CIO publication carried the following observation:

Attempts to change the professional's attitude have been going on for many years. No less eminent a scientist than Albert Einstein spoke in favor of unions for "intellectual workers" 30 years ago. More recently, Nobel laureates Linus Pauling and Harold Urey wrote in support of unionization among scientists.[9]

Thus far this advice has not been followed.

College Faculties. More than 800,000 individuals are employed as college and university members. There is substantial organization among them, split three ways. The oldest group is the American Association of University Professors, which helps its members by publishing annual data and salaries and by policing gross violations of professorial rights, particularly breaches of tenure. The American Federation of Teachers and the National Education Association are bargaining organizations. They have done best in the larger public universities, where political pressure can be generated against university administrators. The large state universities of New York and California are good examples. But they have had less success with the large, prestigious private universities such as the Ivy League, and with small private colleges.

Faculty unions face an important obstacle in the 1980 Yeshiva decision of the U.S. Supreme Court in which the court held that faculty members of private institutions were essentially managers and therefore not protected by the National Labor Relation Act. Colleges can thus openly oppose organization of their faculties and refuse to bargain with them without running the risk of being held to account for an unfair labor practice. There has also been a dilution of faculties by the employment of part-time teachers and the widespread use of teaching assistants, some of whom have attempted unionization on their own.

The substantial organization that already exists among college faculties suggests that this may be a fertile field for the unions. Universities are facing pressure from rising costs on the one hand and a rebellion against mounting tuition on the other. If they attempt to resolve the problem by reducing the real salaries of professors or instituting staff cuts, they may make good targets.

NOTES

1. See Richard B. Freeman and Casey Ichniowski, *When Public Sector Workers Unionize* (Chicago: University of Chicago Press, 1988), pp. 365–397.

2. AFL-CIO Public Employees Department, *Public Employees: Facts and Figures*, 1993, pp. 36–37.

3. Jeffrey S. Zax and Casey Ichniowski, "Bargaining Laws and Unionization in the Local Public Sector," *Industrial and Labor Relations Review* (April 1990), p. 447.

4. Peter Feuille, "Unionism in the Public Sector: the Joy of Protected Markets," *Journal of Labor Research* (Fall 1991), p. 358.

5. Sar A. Levitan and Frank Gallo, "Collective Bargaining and Private Sector Professionals," *Monthly Labor Review* (September 1989), p. 24.

6. For a brief history of this organization see Herbert R. Northrup, Theresa Diss Greis, and Kay M. Dowgun, "The Office and Employees International Union," *Journal of Labor Research* (Winter 1988), p. 91; *Journal of Labor Research* (Summer 1988), p. 25.

7. AFL-CIO, Department for Professional Employees, *Professional Workers and Unions*, June 1988, p. 32.

8. Geoffrey Latta, "Union Organization Among Engineers," *Industrial and Labor*

Relations Review (October 1981), pp. 29–42; Levitan and Gallo, "Collective Bargaining and Private Sector Professionals," pp. 29–30.

9. Dennis Chamot, AFL-CIO, "Scientists and Unions: the New Reality," *American Federationist* (September 1974), p. 12.

CHAPTER 12

Political Action

The merged labor movement has been heavily engaged in politics throughout its existence, both on the national and state levels. Through the Committee on Political Education (COPE) it has endorsed candidates for political office, helped finance their campaigns, and provided other types of assistance. The AFL-CIO and many of its affiliates maintain lobbyists in Washington and state capitals to further their legislative and administrative objectives. Political action committees (PACs) raise election funds and distribute them subject to legal constraints. The Federation is not the most important fund raiser in Washington, but its political backing is not a negligible factor and is sought by politicians who are willing to give some support to its programs.

This chapter presents a discussion of trade union political activities. First there is a chronology of the candidates who were favored in the presidential elections since the merger. The occupant of the White House is in a position to advance the union agenda or to block it. Only once since 1956 has the AFL-CIO as an organization failed to endorse a candidate. The second portion of the chapter is devoted to the question of the extent to which the unions have motivated their members to vote along lines that they advocate, and to the magnitude of the resources committed by the affiliated unions for electoral purposes.

PRESIDENTIAL ELECTIONS

A few words are in order about how the AFL-CIO, as distinct from its affiliates, chooses candidates to support. Under the scheme originally adopted the Executive Council, by majority vote, made a recommendation to the General Board, which then made the final decision. In fact, the Council's recommendation was tantamount to an endorsement, given the fact that its members included the heads of all the major unions. There were some complaints that this was undemocratic in centering decision-making on a few top leaders, and it was later modified to allow for more rank and file input.

It is important to note that an affiliated union is under no obligation to follow the lead of the AFL-CIO. It is fully at liberty to support a candidate of its own choosing, before or during primary elections and after the AFL-CIO has taken a position. AFL-CIO procedures are voluntary and can be disregarded without penalty. There have been elections in which unity was achieved and others in which affiliates went their own way. How a union acts depends a great deal on its perception of its own interests. There is also the factor of rank-and-file opinion; a union leader would not want to act against deeply held views of his members, and these may reflect social values distinct from narrower union concerns. Voting by ethnic groups is one example of a possible source of conflict.

1956. There was not a unanimous union position on Dwight Eisenhower versus Adlai Stevenson. A motion to endorse a presidential candidate was carried in the Executive Council by a vote of 14–8, followed by a 17–5 endorsement of Stevenson. The Council minutes do not reveal how individual members voted, but George Meany's biographer reported that Meany opposed Stevenson on the ground that he had failed to take a sufficiently clear stand on school desegregation.[1] Of the fourteen members in favor of making an endorsement, the opposition to Stevenson came from former AFL leaders, while the pro-Stevenson group was split between the AFL and CIO.

1960. Again, there was no unanimity in the choice of a presidential candidate. John F. Kennedy had been a member of the McClellan Committee and Robert Kennedy had been its assiduous general counsel. When the Kennedy name came up at the 1959 AFL-CIO convention, Michael Quill, head of the Transport Workers Union, declared:

we have got to do some serious thinking as to how much longer we will go along with it, with the Democratic Party, with McClellan and Senator Kennedy, etc. . . . The Kennedy brothers did just as much as Goldwater and Mundt in their attempt to hang, draw, and quarter labor in this last session.[2]

At an August 1960, meeting of the Executive Council, Meany remarked that labor had to take a stand in the forthcoming election and might have to think of the possibility of a labor party if progress could not be made through the two major parties. A. Philip Randolph spoke against any endorsement, while former CIO leaders, including Walter Reuther, favored the Kennedy-Johnson ticket, and the General Board agreed with them. The AFL-CIO had remained neutral at the Democratic Convention, where Johnson and Humphrey were among the candidates, but went all out for Kennedy in the election. There was less than enthusiastic support of the vice-presidential candidate, Lyndon Johnson. Arthur Goldberg, who was close to the Kennedys, had a great deal to do with lining up his ex-CIO colleagues for them.

1964. The Republican nominee, Barry Goldwater, had a near zero voting record in the Senate by labor's tally. Johnson's relations with the AFL-CIO had been satisfactory during his two years in office; he did his best to cultivate the unions. The Executive Council recommended unanimously that the Johnson-Humphrey ticket be endorsed, and the General Board did the same. Maurice Hutcheson, president of the Carpenters Union, said that this was the first time in his life that he agreed to endorse a Democratic presidential candidate. His father, William L. Hutcheson, his predecessor as head of the union, was a life-long Republican and one-time chairman of the Republican Labor Committee.

Johnson carried all but six states. Organized labor spoke with one voice and COPE received generous credit for its contribution to his victory. Sixty-eight percent of Congressional candidates backed by Cope were elected, compared with 57 percent in 1960. This was one of labor's most successful political campaigns.

1968. The 1966 Congressional elections were a harbinger of things to come. COPE devoted a good deal of money and time to support Democrats, but the Republicans gained heavily, which the director of COPE attributed to factional strife within the Democratic Party over the Vietnam war. Senator Paul Douglas, a leading liberal, was defeated, and Ronald Reagan was elected governor of California. Labor acknowledged that it could never muster more than a minority of votes, but that in a close situation it could provide the margin of victory.[3]

Johnson's surprise announcement that he would not run for re-election upset labor's plans to support him once again. Meany urged Vice-President Hubert Humphrey, who was very close to the labor movement, to declare his candidacy. Humphrey won the Democratic nomination, but the disorder at the convention in Chicago reduced his chances. A National Labor Committee for Humphrey was formed, including most of the top AFL-CIO leaders.

One of the problems contributing to Nixon's close victory was the third-party candidacy of George Wallace. COPE reported several months before the election that 30 percent of union members intended to vote for him. Every effort was made to change their minds and many were persuaded to switch to Humphrey. COPE criticized the Democratic Party for failing to develop any real organization in many parts of the country.

1972. This year marked the low point in AFL-CIO presidential campaign participation. Most of the four hundred trade unionists who were delegates to the Democratic convention were supporters of Humphrey or Edmund Muskie; they switched to Henry Jackson when it became clear that the first two did not have the votes. I. W. Abel, the head of the Steelworkers Union, seconded the Jackson nomination. George McGovern, the candidate of the antiwar activists and of minority groups, carried the day. His platform included cessation of bombing and unconditional withdrawal from Vietnam.

The conservative members of the Executive Council pointed to a number of flaws in his senatorial voting record: He voted against cutting off debate on Section 14b of the Taft-Hartley Act; he favored defense cutbacks; he opposed the wheat embargo directed at the Soviet Union. On the other hand, he had an impeccable pro-labor record apart from these positions. The Executive Council decided by a margin of 27 to 3 to refrain from endorsing either Nixon or Mc-Govern, leaving it to individual unions to do as they liked. The three Council members who favored McGovern were Wurf of AFSCME, Alvin Grospiron of the Oil Workers, and Paul Jennings of the Electrical, Radio, and Machine Workers. It will be recalled that the Auto Workers were outside the AFL-CIO at this time.

A number of other unions worked in the McGovern campaign, including the Lithographers, the Transport Workers, the Clothing Workers, the Retail Clerks, the Communications Workers, the Machinists, and the Rubber Workers. Nine building trade unions endorsed Nixon, although the largest one, the Carpenters, remained neutral. The Colorado State Labor Council came out for McGovern, whereupon its charter was suspended by the Executive Council, a decision that was sustained by the 1973 AFL-CIO convention.

The majority group in the Council looked upon McGovern as too far to the left. Meany characterized him as ''an apologist for the Communist world.'' But Nixon's reelection was no victory for the labor movement. The split helped reduce its image as a political force to be reckoned with that it had earned in previous campaigns. Nixon won 50 percent of the union household vote, compared with 47 percent for McGovern. COPE remained silent.

1976. With Watergate and the veto by President Gerald Ford of the situs picketing bill behind them, the unions returned to their usual pattern of national political activity. The Council endorsed the Jimmy Carter–Walter Mondale ticket unanimously. Meany explained why:

We will give [Carter] all-out support of the AFL-CIO. We'll give him all the support that we can legally and legitimately give him through our COPE organization, through our national unions, through our COPE area committees—the entire bit. And the reason I say it will be all-out support is the fact that I cannot find anyone, at any level, in the official family of the American labor movement who is going to be for Gerald Ford.[4]

Meany was as good as his word. In an election in which Carter received only 51 percent of the popular vote, 70 percent of union members voted for him. The AFL-CIO regained some of its prestige and felt entitled to some reward during the next four years.

1980. The euphoria did not last long, and by the time of the 1980 elections some of the controversial actions of the Carter administration had weakened union unanimity. Given the Republican nominee, Ronald Reagan, labor had little option but to support Carter once again. Lane Kirkland termed the Republican platform as devious and disturbing. The Democratic platform was praised for its commitment to raise the minimum wage, to protect the Davis-Bacon Act, to extend the duration of unemployment benefits, and to repeal section 14b of the labor relations law. However, several members of the Executive Council voted in the negative, including William Winpisinger of the Machinists, John O'Donnell of the Airline Pilots, and Fred Kroll of the Railway Clerks. Wurf sent word that he would have abstained had he been at the meeting. The General Board endorsed Carter without dissent, and when he visited their meeting he promised to stand shoulder to shoulder with the unions to restore full employment. The Typographical Union endorsed a presidential candidate for the first time in its history.

In commenting on the outcome of the election at the 1981 AFL-CIO convention, Kirkland had this to say: "Nothing is to be gained from minimizing the results of the 1980 elections. Ronald Reagan won the White House because the American people lost confidence in their Government's ability to handle the nation's mounting domestic and international problems."[5] Reagan carried 44 states and the Republicans gained control of the Senate. COPE had not done a bad job in getting the vote out; 58 percent of AFL-CIO members who had cast their ballots voted for Carter, 17 percent more than in the electorate at large. Some 65 percent of union members had voted, compared with 52 percent of the general public. But this was not sufficient to overcome Carter's unpopularity, ascribed variously to inflation, unemployment, and foreign policy failures.

1984. Carter had never been an ideal presidential candidate from the union point of view. He was simply accepted as the Democratic nominee. It gradually occurred to the leadership that putting their weight behind candidates in primary elections might be a better way of ensuring their choice. The problem was that individual unions had their own favorites, making it difficult to reach unity at so early a stage.

In preparation for the 1984 elections, the General Board adopted a set of rules that it hoped would solve this problem. Board endorsement would require a two-thirds vote of all the votes cast, including nonendorsement and abstention. The voting strength of each union represented would be based on its membership at the previous AFL-CIO convention. There would be a maximum of two ballots, and if no primary candidate received two-thirds of the vote on the first ballot, there would be a runoff between the two top scorers. If there were still no two-thirds majority, there would be no endorsement.

This scheme had its first test in October 1963, when Walter Mondale was endorsed for the 1984 campaign. He received 90.7 percent of the Board vote, John Glenn 3.3 percent, while the rest went for no endorsement. Mondale had been close to the unions while he was Vice-President and his popularity carried over. As the primaries heated up, one of the contestants, Gary Hart, portrayed Mondale as beholden to "special interests," using the Board endorsement as evidence. The unions found Hart's voting record wanting, and later welcomed the selection of Geraldine Ferraro as vice-presidential candidate, citing her strong pro-union voting record as a member of the House of Representatives.

The AFL-CIO commissioned an exit poll to determine how its members had voted. The results indicated that 61 percent of AFL-CIO members had voted for Mondale, compared with 41 percent of the electorate as a whole. Union women were more prone than men to support Mondale, 68 versus 58 percent. There was no comfort in the magnitude of the Reagan landslide, but the unions found some hope in the conclusion that:

although the Republicans have made some gains among certain subgroups of union members as the party best able to deal with defense issues, social questions, the deficit and, to a lesser degree, the economy, President Reagan faces great resistance from union members on most of the domestic initiatives now being considered by his Administration.[6]

1988. The endorsement procedure in 1988 did not go as smoothly as it had in 1984. The General Board was unable to reach a consensus during the primaries. The Council urged the delegates to the AFL-CIO 1987 convention not to make any endorsement before the Federation had acted, and suggested that union officers and staffers refrain from supplying money to or acting on behalf of any of the contenders in order to preserve labor unity. Not until Michael Dukakis was nominated by the Democratic convention did the AFL-C10 make its choice. When the General Board was polled not a single union backed Bush, although several abstained on the ground that they had not finished polling their members. One of the unions that abstained was the newly affiliated Teamsters Union, which eventually came out for Bush.

An exit poll revealed that 69 percent of AFL-CIO members had voted for Dukakis against 31 percent for Bush. The respondents reported that during several months before the election, 80 percent had been contacted by a union, 65 percent by phone, and the rest by mail or personal contact. When asked to indicate the single most important issue that had influenced their decisions, the answer was the economy, but not by a large margin. On their sources of information, television came first with 28 percent, newspapers followed with 25 percent, and only 8 percent cited the unions. Workers in manufacturing supplied the largest majority for Dukakis, and those in service occupations, the lowest.[7] In his report on the campaign to the 1989 AFL-CIO convention, Kirkland stated:

This was not a case of telling union members how to vote. Rather it was a case of union members giving their federation its marching orders, through their unions, after a thoroughly democratic process. The goal of endorsement was and is secondary to the primary objective of labor unity in political action.[8]

1992. After twelve years in the wilderness the labor movement emerged victorious in 1992. To further focus its efforts, the Federation had decided at its 1991 convention to refine the endorsement procedure on the basis of the following voluntary guidelines:

1. Unions should not make any public endorsements of candidates until the General Board has acted according to existing guidelines.

2. Union officers and staff should not participate in committees or raise funds on behalf of potential candidates, but they can provide funds to announced candidates prior to AFL-CIO endorsements.

3. Equal courtesy and accommodation should be extended to all announced candidates.

4. Unions are urged to use their own methods of determining the preferences of their members.

5. Each 1991 national and political event should be reviewed case by case.

6. The purpose of the guidelines is to maintain labor unity. If it is apparent that consensus exists, the General Board will be assembled to determine whether there is a two-thirds majority.[9]

In March 1992, the Executive Council voted to release unions to work for primary candidates. Of thirty-two Council members polled, fourteen said they were prepared to vote for Harkin, three for Clinton (AFSCME, Retail, and Teachers), while the rest were uncommitted. Nine members, mainly from the old CIO, set up a committee for Harkin, whom they regarded as the most liberal candidate.

Six Democratic candidates were invited to hold a forum at the 1991 AFL-CIO convention—Kerry, Clinton, Brown, Wilder, Harkin, and Tsongas. Clinton came out for a "tough and fair" trade policy, affordable health care, lifetime training opportunities, public investment in infrastructure, funding for Head Start, a national system of apprenticeship, lower interest rates on credit cards, and home mortgage insurance. He made one comment that went right to the heart of union concerns: "I don't think it's fair to say workers have a right to strike and say that means the right to lose your job."[10] Eventually both the Council and the Board endorsed Clinton almost unanimously. For the first time in twenty years the Teamsters endorsed a Democrat.

The exit polls in the final elections showed that 60 percent of union households cast their ballots for Clinton, well above the general rate. Union activity was particularly important in some of the industrial states, where the unions delivered the margin of victory. On election day more than 300,000 union members participated in efforts to get out the union vote. The reward? Lane Kirkland stated: "working Americans now have good reason to expect that government will be back on their side where it rightfully belongs, working with them in the awesome task of rebuilding our industries, our standard of living and our ideals."[11]

THE EFFECTIVENESS AND MAGNITUDE OF POLITICAL ACTION

There have been several extensive analyses of how effective political action has been in furthering union objectives. One of the most comprehensive, by

Table 12.1
Trade Union Political Action Committee Activity, 1977–1988

Election cycle	Unions with PACs	Union PAC Disbursements (thousands of dollars)	Union PAC Disbursements (thousands of 1977–78 dollars)
1977–78	72	18,638	18,538
1979–80	80	25,100	20,917
1981–82	78	34,813	23,209
1983–84	83	47,544	28,990
1985–86	82	57,882	32,888
1987–88	na	70,428	37,663

Source: John Thomas Delaney and Marick F. Masters, "Unions and Political Action," in George Strauss et al., *The State of the Unions* (Madison, WI: Industrial Relations Research Association, 1990), p. 320.

Masters and Delaney, covers the period 1948 to 1984, based on findings of over sixty studies. Some of the most interesting conclusions are the following:

1. A majority of union members support their unions' political activities, although between 20 and 45 percent have some reservations about specific union policies.
2. Union members tend to vote Democratic more than nonmembers, although there has been some erosion of this split over time.
3. Most major unions maintain staffs of lobbyists in Washington, although they are clearly outnumbered by corporate lobbyists.
4. "Union members perceive union leaders as being out of touch with the rank and file on political matters. Union officials may be caught in the middle, with members willing to support political action aimed at labor relations legislation and legislators preferring the political safety of voting for bills that do not directly strengthen unions."[12]

Unions are forbidden by federal law from using dues money for the support of presidential and congressional nominees. However, they may establish political action committees funded by voluntary member contributions, and most of them have done so. The amounts involved are shown in Table 12.1 for two-year election periods from 1977 to 1988, both in current and constant dollars. The expenditures outran the inflation, doubling during the decade. In the magnitude of their contributions, the Auto Workers and the Machinists led the way.

Financial support is only one index of union commitment to political action. Nonmonetary services such as manning telephone banks, distributing literature, ringing doorbells, and performing other tasks for election committees may actually be of more assistance to candidates than cash. On the other hand, the

Table 12.2
Election Victories Won by AFL-CIO Endorsed Candidates in Elections with Endorsed Candidates (percent)[a]

Year	House of Representatives	Senate
1978	69.2	40.0
1980	62.0	34.4
1982	63.8	64.5
1984	63.5	53.6
1986	66.6	67.9
1988	69.9	60.0

[a]The figures in this table and those cited in the text are drawn from different sources and do not always agree.

Source: John Thomas Delaney and Marick F. Masters, "Unions and Political Action," in George Strauss et al., *The State of the Unions* (Madison, WI: Industrial Relations Research Association, 1990), p. 326.

growing importance of television for electioneering has been raising the importance of financial contributions.

A good deal of COPE activity is directed to elections for the House of Representatives and the Senate. Some idea of union success in this area can be gained from the data in Table 12.2. Roughly two-thirds of COPE-endorsed candidates for House seats tended to win fairly constantly, while there was greater variability in the Senate races. It is important to remember, however, that COPE assistance did not necessarily guarantee union success in achieving its legislative objectives. The AFL-CIO is only one of a number of constituencies that congressmen must satisfy, and often not the most important. Moreover, the box-score of votes that provides the basis for selective endorsements includes a number of issues that are not of specific concern to union members—tax policy, education, energy, social security, foreclosure relief, among others. Even so-called labor issues do not all involve narrow trade union interests. Congressmen also have the problem of whether to vote at the behest of the party whip, though the relative independence of American congressmen makes this less important than in European parliamentary systems.

The extent to which the unions have supported the Democratic Party is illustrated by the data in Table 12.3. Apart from the 1972 election, more than half of union members voted for the Democratic presidential candidate, and in some cases many more than half, while nonunion voters were consistently below half except for the 1964 Johnson landslide. Both groups were more Democratically inclined in the congressional races, but the gap between the two persisted. In neither case, however, were union voters unanimous. A sizable minority of them voted Republican.

Despite a mixed record of success, the AFL-CIO has placed more emphasis

Table 12.3
Democratic Party Share of Votes, Union and Nonunion, 1956–1988 (percent)[a]

Year	Presidential vote		Congressional vote	
	Union	*Nonunion*	*Union*	*Nonunion*
1956	53	36	62	49
1960	64	44	69	51
1964	83	62	80	59
1968	56	43	58	50
1972	43	33	62	53
1976	64	47	72	52
1980	55	40	65	51
1984	57	37	62	53
1988	59	46	na	na

[a]The figures in this table and those cited in the text are drawn from different sources and do not
always agree.
Source: John Thomas Delaney and Marick F. Masters, "Unions and Political Action," in George
Strauss et al., *The State of the Unions* (Madison, WI: Industrial Relations Research Association,
1990), p. 332.

on political action over time. There were long periods of discouragement, but
the years of Kennedy, Johnson, Carter, and Clinton opened up vistas of hope.
The unions are wedded to the political arena because they have no choice. The
political atmosphere is crucial to their success or failure in collective bargaining.
A friend in the White House can help them in many ways, formally and infor-
mally.

NOTES

1. Archie Robinson, *George Meany and His Times* (New York: Simon and Schuster,
1981), p. 209.
2. AFL-CIO, *Proceedings of the Third Constitutional Convention*, 1959, p. 384.
3. AFL-CIO, *Minutes of the Executive Council*, February 27, 1967, p. 91.
4. Press Conference, quoted in Robinson, *George Meany and His Times*, p. 347.
5. AFL-CIO, *Report of the Executive Council to the Fourteenth Constitutional Convention*, 1981, p. 2.
6. AFL-CIO, "How AFL-CIO Members Voted in the 1984 Elections," *The American Federationist* (December 1, 1984), p. 8.
7. *AFL-CIO News*, December 3, 1988, p. 8.
8. AFL-CIO, *Report of the Executive Council to the Eighteenth Constitutional Convention.* 1989, p. 3.
9. AFL-CIO, *Proceedings of the Nineteenth Constitutional Convention*, 1991, p. 219.
10. Ibid., p. 170.

11. Lane Kirkland in AFL-CIO, *Report of the Executive Council to the Twentieth Constitutional Convention*, 1993, p. 1.

12. Marick F. Masters and John Thomas Delaney, "Union Political Activities: A Review of the Empirical Literature," *Industrial and Labor Relations Review* (April 1987), pp. 337–351.

CHAPTER 13

Labor and the Law

The trade unions attribute a good part of their recent difficulties to the legal environment in which they operate. They cite not only the two major pieces of postwar legislation—The Taft-Hartley Act and the Landrum Griffin Act—but also the interpretation and administration of the legislation by the NLRB and the courts. The NLRB is normally the first to deal with violations, but the courts are the final arbiters of what is permitted in industrial relations.

It is impracticable to deal here with the many cases that arise each year at the various levels of adjudication. The reader who is interested in greater depth is urged to consult a textbook on labor law.[1] This chapter reviews the major Supreme Court decisions affecting labor since the time of the merger.

Before dealing with specific cases it may be useful to look at the attitudes of the Supreme Court during this period. Was it friendly or hostile? Did it favor unions or employers? A good source for examining these issues is the reports of the AFL-CIO legal department to the biennial conventions. These reports summarize relevant Court decisions and are often prefaced by brief evaluations of its labor posture.[2]

1961. "The last two years of litigation in the Supreme Court produced the greatest string of victories for the labor movement in recent history. All told, two dozen major decisions netted a winning percentage of better than 800." (p. 186)

1963. "About two dozen important legal propositions were established by the 1962 and 1963 Supreme Court decisions. A full two-thirds of them represented victories for the views of organized labor." (p. 189)

1965. "Unions posted an exceptional won-lost record in the unusually large batch of labor cases which were considered by the Supreme Court during the past two years. Of some twenty-eight significant decisions, twenty can be scored as labor victories.'' (p. 166)

1967. ''While some reverses were incurred in the cases that were decided, unions continued to maintain a good overall won-lost record and to score a number of major successes. The Court's past term, which saw seven clear union victories and no important clear losses in 10 decided cases, several establishing important new principles, will hopefully be a portent of the future.'' (p. 167)

1969. ''The final two terms of the Warren Court were highly successful from the labor point of view. The Court considered 22 cases and labor prevailed in 15. Given the Court's activist liberal stance, the labor-management field provided the bulk of the triumphs, and the regulation of the union-member relationship was the major source of the few setbacks which were suffered.'' (p. 169)

1971. With the retirement of Justices Warren and Abe Fortas and the appointment of Chief Justice Warren Burger, the tide began to turn. The Nixon appointees to the Court (Burger and Blackmun) were ''fundamentally unsympathetic to the views of organized labor at least in regard to labor-management disputes. One or two additional justices of a similar persuasion would present the union movement with a problem of the first magnitude.'' (p. 198)

1973. That these fears were well founded emerges from assessment of Supreme Court decisions during the next two years. The basic lesson was ''that it is unrealistic to expect major legal advances by organized labor within the foreseeable future. The most that can be anticipated is a series of hard fought struggles some successful, some not, to maintain the far from satisfactory status quo.'' (p. 234)

1975. The full impact of the four Court members appointed by Nixon was becoming clear. ''The last two years have produced few important decisions favorable to the labor movement and many whose effect will be seriously detrimental. . . . The results of 33 of the 44 decided cases impinging on the rights of employees and of unions can be said to be favorable or unfavorable. Only 11 were in any sense union victories. But the statistics underrepresent the extent of the losses sustained. Many of the defeats were on matters that have important ramifications for the future of organized labor. . . . the Court is subject to indictment both for the results it reached and for the methods it too often employed to reach those results.'' (p. 222)

1977. The Legal Department reported that the Court had become more interested in cases involving the rights of public employees and discrimination, and less in the area of labor relations. This was considered helpful for ''the Court as presently constituted seems disposed, when it does decide important cases in this area, to decide against the union position.'' (p. 304)

1979. ''. . . public employees . . . are—mercifully, given the dismal record of most recent cases—no longer receiving a great deal of Supreme Court attention.'' As for labor-management, there was ''a decided blurring of the plainly anti-organized labor trend of recent years. . . . This is certainly not to say that the present Court is generally favorable to the concerns of organized labor. . . . Rather, as the Supreme Court labor docket shifts into areas less focused upon union activity as such, the decisions in employment related cases seem somewhat more dispassionate." (p. 290)

1981. A moderate trend continued, with more interest in collective bargaining. The unions won 19 of 28 cases in that area. But the statistics were misleading, for "unions were simply able to stave off legal attacks upon their interests and those of employees." (p. 258)

1983. "The present justices of the Supreme Court are invulnerable to any accusation of being motivated by a partiality to organized labor. Yet during the past two years the labor movement more than held its own in the Court. Of the 41 cases in which a union was a party or in which the AFL-CIO participated as an *amicus curiae* that produced a clear cut decision, the union prevailed in 27 and the union position was rejected in 14." A new Court appointee, Justice Sandra Day O'Connor had "indicated a marked antipathy for the legal positions urged by unions, ruling against the union position in each of the Court's unanimous labor relations cases." (pp. 258–259)

1985. The dearth of labor cases during the two previous years was attributed to the waning influence of federal law in setting the balance of power between labor and management. The NLRB had become so hostile to unions that the latter were not invoking legal protection but relying instead on self-help. "At the same time the present Court's few significant decisions have been a contributing factor to this sequence of events. For the Burger court has been at its most ideological in dealing with conflicts between labor and management, and the interests of workers are particularly unlikely to prevail when those employees seek to express their interests through concerted activity against management." (pp. 273–274)

1987. Of the cases decided by the Supreme Court in 1986 and 1987, some 21 that were of direct interest to labor were decided in favor of the unions, ten were against them, and 15 produced a mixed result. "The Supreme Court's decisions reveal a more somber meaning: The laws designed to protect and advance the practice and procedure of collective bargaining are not adequate to that task and, as a result, working people are less and less able to directly influence their wages and working conditions and more dependent on direct government regulation of the employment relationship." (p. 292)

1989. The assessment of this period was prefaced by the statement that the labor movement was well justified in helping defeat the nomination of Robert Bork to the Supreme Court. There was a complaint that Anthony Kennedy had aligned himself with the most conservative members of the Court. "The Court now has a working majority of right-wing judicial activists who have no sympathy for the federal laws intended to protect working men and women from overriding employer power." In 1988 and 1989, two-thirds of the cases decided by the Court went against unions or individual employees. "These trends suggest that the Rehnquist court may be on the verge of doing to the nation's civil rights what the Burger and Rehnquist courts have already done to our labor laws.'' (pp. 285–286)

1991. Workers and unions did well in the 16 labor-management cases decided in 1990 and 1991. ''But looking behind the results at why the cases came out as they did shows no cause for celebration. . . . the fact that the labor movement did as well as it has should not be taken as an indication that the labor law is developing in a favorable way. The trend is a source of some satisfaction only to the extent it reflects the Court's disposition not to push the adverse development of the labor law beyond its current path, and not to accept the arguments of the employers and right-wing zealots who agitate for even more anti-worker, anti-union results.'' (pp. 280–281)

1993. The approximately 50–50 record of the two previous years ''must be understood as reflecting a mix of equivocal victories and unequivocal defeats'' for the unions. The ''centrist'' group of justices, O'Connor, Kennedy, and Souter, is a ''profoundly conservative center'' according to the union lawyers. It was too soon to have any reaction to the Clinton appointees. (p. 297)

From the labor point of view, the Warren court came out by far the best, with one mixed and five good ratings. The Burger court had only one good rating, four mixed, and two bad, and the Rehnquist court was about the same. For the half century since the merger, the labor movement did not face an overwhelmingly hostile Court, on the basis of these evaluations—nothing like the Supreme Court of pre–New Deal years. But the trend since 1955 was clearly against what labor perceived as its interests. Warren to Burger to Rehnquist represented a downward slope.

ORGANIZING ACTIVITIES

A union must have access to employees if it is to organize them. This may take the form of picketing the employer's place of business, distributing handbills, or engaging employees in conversation. Radio broadcasting is no longer very productive, and television is expensive.

There has been a long series of cases delineating where and in what manner these activities may be carried on. Access to company property may be involved, as well as the right of free speech. A 1945 case held it an unfair labor practice for an employer to deny a union access to its premises after working hours for the purpose of contacting employees. This was later modified to permit restriction of access if the location of a plant and the living quarters of employees did not deprive the union of the opportunity of approaching employees by making reasonable efforts to do so.

A difficult problem arises with respect to private property, such as shopping malls, that is open to the public. The question in *Central Hardware v. NLRB* was whether a union could solicit employees on the parking lot of a retail store. The ruling was against the union.[3] The most recent case in a long procession of lawsuits on this issue came in 1992 in a landmark decision, *Lechmere v.*

NLRB.[4] Lechmere operated a chain of retail stores. The United Food Workers began an organizing campaign among its employees in Newington, Connecticut. It placed ads in a local paper and put handbills on the windshields of employees' cars parked in an adjoining lot. The company claimed that it had barred any solicitation by all groups and removed the handbills, and asked organizers to leave. The union picketed elsewhere, distributed handbills to employees as they entered the parking lot, noted their license numbers, and followed up with mailings and home visits. All this resulted in only a single union authorization card.

The union then filed unfair labor practice charges, claiming that it did not have adequate access, and the NLRB sustained the complaint. The Supreme Court reversed in a 5–3 decision. Writing for the majority, Justice Clarence Thomas held that if there were any alternative means of communication away from the employer's property, including signs across a grassy strip along a major highway contiguous to the store, the union could be barred from the employer's property.

A study of this line of cases reached the following conclusion:

The Supreme Court's decision in Lechmere was a major victory for employers. . . . The Lechmere decision may help curtail some of the increasingly aggressive tactics that some unions have used in recruiting campaigns. . . . For unions, the Lechmere decision was a step backward. The modern retail workplace is replete with a plethora of malls, office buildings, and shopping plazas surrounded by private property. Unlike manufacturing and wholesale concerns, few retailers are situated today in a single building on a traditional Main Street with a public sidewalk The access to retail employees is frequently limited. With the Lechmere decision, unions will need to find more innovative means of making personal contact. This may include resorting to prohibitively expensive means of solicitation such as television advertising.[5]

Secondary picketing is a tactic used by unions as a way of putting pressure on an employer. What this means is getting at the primary employer, whose employees the union is attempting to organize, by picketing employers with whom he has business relationships. This is basically prohibited by Taft-Hartley. However, what happens when a craft union pickets a construction site in a dispute with a contractor working on a job, which inevitably involves pressure on other crafts at the same site? In a 1951 decision the Supreme Court ruled that this constituted an illegal secondary boycott, leading to a forty-year effort by the construction unions to reverse this decision by legislation—the unsuccessful situs picketing quest.

Another important secondary boycott case turned out differently. The Teamsters Union had called a strike against fruit packers in the State of Washington and picketed several Safeway stores in Seattle that were selling the packer's apples. The Supreme Court ruled that Congress had not intended to forbid picketing in front of a secondary retail establishment asking customers not to purchase certain apples, but not asking them to refrain from buying other commodities.[6] The unions won another victory when they were permitted to distribute handbills in a shopping mall publicizing a dispute with a construction company that was building a department store there, urging shoppers not to buy in the mall.[7]

Persuading an employer to recognize a union can be a difficult phase of an organizing campaign. Is it necessary to win an NLRB election, or is presentation of an adequate number of signed authorization cards sufficient? The Warren court held that such presentation was sufficient, provided the cards were obtained from a majority of the employees in the bargaining unit without misrepresentation or coercion.[8] This decision has enabled unions to bypass the lengthy election procedures of the NLRB on occasion.

EMPLOYEE TACTICS

The Warren court refused to label a slowdown of work preparatory to bargaining an unfair labor practice, holding that the ''presence of economic weapons in reserve and their actual exercise on occasion by the parties is part and parcel of the system that the Wagner and Taft-Hartley Acts have recognized.''[9] But the Court has ruled that it was an unfair labor practice to distribute handbills that attacked the quality of an employer's television broadcasts without referring to the existence of a labor dispute. However, boycott signs during a dispute have generally been protected.

STRIKES AND THEIR CONSEQUENCES

Strikes have become one of the most controversial aspects of labor law because of their practical consequences. The controversy stems from a 1938 Supreme Court decision in which it was held that strikebreakers could permanently replace strikers provided that the strike was not caused by the employer's unfair labor practice.[10] The Court has limited the application of this doctrine in several ways. Where a strike was called off and the strikers sought reinstatement before a full crew had been hired, the Court ruled that it was an unfair labor practice to hire new employees before offering reinstatement to the strikers.[11] On the other hand, the Rehnquist court allowed TWA to assign less-senior flight attendants who had gone through picket lines to more desirable jobs when the strike was over, thus destroying the seniority rights of the reurning strikers.[12]

COLLECTIVE BARGAINING

In a landmark case decided in 1959, the Court set out three types of subjects that might be introduced at the bargaining table by either party: mandatory, nonmandatory, and illegal. Refusal to bargain to an impasse on a mandatory issue could be an unfair labor practice. Insistence on continued bargaining on a nonmandatory issue could also be unfair, as would be the introduction of an illegal issue. In the Borg Warner case the Court ruled that an employer's refusal to enter into a contract unless it included a "ballot" clause calling for a prestrike vote on the employer's last offer and a "recognition" clause that excluded the national union that had been certified as a bargaining agent constituted a refusal to bargain in that these were nonmandatory subjects.[13]

The Court has sought in a number of cases to sort out the status of various collective bargaining issues. In one, it held that the employer could insist on the right to contract work out. On the other hand, the Court left undisturbed a lower court decision that the insistence by a company on staying with a "take it or leave it" offer did not constitute good faith bargaining. In general, it does not appear that unions have been unduly hampered by this line of decisions.

UNION REPRESENTATION OBLIGATIONS

Unlike the practice in many countries, American law provides that there can be only one representative of the employees in an appropriate bargaining unit, the organization that speaks for the majority of the employees. There is a correlative obligation for the organization that gains this status to represent all the employees in the unit with equal fairness whether or not they are members.

In a leading case the Supreme Court held that a union did not violate its obligation by settling a grievance unfavorably to the grievant before the final arbitration stage of the contract procedure.[14] This means that in some sense the grievance belongs to the union, and may be handled by the union as long as it is acting in good faith. Another important case was handed down at the same session of the Court dealing with the responsibility of the union for the acts of its members. The Court held that an injunction could be used against the union only if there were clear proof that violent acts committed by its members were participated in, authorized by, or ratified by the union.[15]

Another union victory was won in a case involving a challenge to a union's settlement of a strike on the ground that it violated the rights of dissenting members of the bargaining unit. It was ruled here that unions have broad discretion in determining the best interests of those it represents unless it can be shown to have acted in bad faith.[16]

The duty to represent may also call into question the ability of unions to discipline members who violate its statutes. The general rule established was that members and those working under an agency shop agreement were obliged only to pay initiation fees and dues. The Court ruled, however, that a union could exact a reasonable fine from strikebreakers who crossed picket lines.[17] On the other hand, a union member who resigned during a strike and returned to work while the strike was still on was not subject to discipline.[18] This opened a hole in the enforcement of union discipline.

INTERNAL AFFAIRS OF UNIONS

The Landrum-Griffin Act prescribed a bill of rights for union members. Precisely what it entailed had to be adjudicated by the courts. A leading case involved a bitter leadership struggle in the Steelworkers Union between the incumbents and a dissident group headed by Edward Sadlowski. Following an unsuccessful bid for the presidency by Sadlowski, the union promulgated a rule prohibiting candidates for union office from receiving contributions of money or time from outside the union. Sadlowski charged that this unduly restricted his right to free speech, but the Court held the rule to be reasonable.[19] The Court also upheld a newly elected local union president who discharged business agents for supporting his opponent, on the theory that Landrum-Griffin protected rank and file members but not officials. Yet a few years later there was a decision that elected officials, as distinct from appointed officials, could not be discharged for opposing incumbents on the ground that this would interfere with the rights of members to choose their leaders.[20]

SUCCESSORSHIP

The Warren court held in 1964 that when a business is sold, the new employer must abide by the terms of a collective agreement that had been in effect before the sale as long as there was a substantial continuity of operations. The Rehnquist court reversed this doctrine eight years later, but it was restored after another five years, an important ruling in a period of mergers and takeovers.[21]

A brief review of Supreme Court cases does not provide the basis for a determination of whether the Court has had a negative impact on the fortunes of the AFL-CIO and its affiliates. That the AFL-CIO believes it has is evident from the summaries of its legal staff. The Federation sought assistance from the Carter administration to correct what it considered to be unfair doctrinal holdings and administrative procedures. The principal elements of the Labor Reform Bill of 1978 that the Federation promoted were the following:

1. Mandatory injunctions issued summarily against certain union unfair labor practices would be extended to discriminatory discharges by employers, thus permitting quick remedial reinstatement.

2. Double back pay would be given to workers illegally discharged for union activity.

3. Compensation would be provided to employees when employers illegally refused to bargain.

4. Wilfull violators of labor laws would be barred from access to federal contracts on authorization of the Secretary of Labor.

The bill passed the House of Representatives by a vote of 257 to 153 after intense lobbying by the AFL-CIO. There was a Democratic majority in the Senate and there were high hopes for final enactment. Business groups waged a massive fight against the legislation, and the end result was a deficiency of two votes that were necessary to invoke cloture.

STATE LEGISLATION

Section 14b of the Taft-Hartley Act, which empowers the states to bar union security agreements despite contrary provisions of the Act, may have been as harmful to union progress as anything else in federal law. Right-to-work laws prohibiting union shop agreements have been adopted by twenty states, including most of the Southern states to which industry has been migrating. These laws make it difficult for unions to recruit and hold recalcitrant workers even where they have exclusive bargaining rights. An econometric study concluded that the enactment of such a law reduced union membership by between 5 and 10 percent.[22]

As noted above, the ability to organize public employees is partly dependent on state legislation governing collective bargaining. No two states have the same laws. Perhaps a dozen states permit strikes by some groups of their employees, always excluding police and fire-fighting personnel. Most states provide for procedures where there are impasses in bargaining, including mediation, fact finding, or arbitration. Final and binding arbitration is the norm in about twenty-five states, but not necessarily for all categories of employees. Apart from the right-to-work laws, state legislation, where it exists, does not appear to have limited union growth in the public sector.

NOTES

1. A good introduction may be found in William B. Gould IV, *A Primer in American Labor Law*, 3d ed. (Cambridge, MA: MIT Press, 1993).

2. The quotations and page numbers in the following section are from AFL-CIO, *Report of the Executive Council to the Biennial Convention* for years indicated in the text.

3. 406 U.S. 535 (1972).

4. 112 S.Ct. 841 (1992).

5. Ellen P. Kelly et al., "*NLRB v. Lechmere:* Union Quest for Access," *Journal of Labor Research* (Spring 1994), p. 166.

6. *NLRB v. Fruit and Vegetable Packers*, 377 U.S. 58 (1964).

7. *Edward J. DeBartolo Corp. v. Florida Gulf Coast Building Trades Council*, 485 U.S. 568 (1988).

8. *NLRB v. Gissel Packing Co.*, 395 U.S. 575 (1969).

9. *NLRB v. Insurance Agents International Union*, 361 U.S. 477 (1960).

10. *NLRB v. Mackay Radio and Telegraph Co.*, 204 U.S. 333 (1938).

11. *NLRB v. Fleetwood Trailer Corp.*, 389 U.S. 375 (1967).

12. *TWA v. Independent Federation of Flight Attendants*, 489 U.S. 426 (1989).

13. *NLRB v. Wooster Division of Borg Warner*, 356 U.S. 347 (1958).

14. *Vaca v. Sipes*, 386 U.S. 190 (1965).

15. *United Mine Workers v. Gibbs*, 383 U.S. 715 (1966).

16. *Air Line Pilots Association v. O'Neill*, 111 S.Ct. 1127 (1991).

17. *NLRB v. Allis Chalmers*, 388 U.S. 175 (1967).

18. *Pattern Makers League v. NLRB*, 473 U.S. 95 (1985).

19. *United Steelworkers v. Sadlowski*, 475 U.S. 102 (1982).

20. *Finnegan v. Leu*, 456 U.S. 431 (1982); *Sheet Metal Workers v. Lynn*, 488 U.S. 347 (1989).

21. *John Wiley & Sons. v. Livingston*, 376 U.S. 543 (1964); *NLRB v Burns*, 406 U.S. 272 (1972).

22. David T. Ellwood and Glen Fine, "The Impact of Right to Work Laws on Union Organizing," *Journal of Political Economy*, vol. 95, no. 2 (1987), p. 271.

CHAPTER 14

Foreign Affairs

Foreign policy issues are normally not considered by most people as directly affecting their well being, so long as there is no disruption of life, as would be true with military action. They do not usually arouse emotions except among ethnic or religious groups whose country of origin may be involved. Determination of union policy on foreign matters is usually left to the leaders, and not all of them at that.

Ideology can be an important factor in the formation of foreign policy. All AFL-CIO leaders have been opposed to communism, but there were differences in the depth of their opposition to it and on the manner in which it should be fought. George Meany had a bedrock antipathy toward communism, while Walter Reuther was a centrist. Reuther was the victor in a bruising struggle against communists in his own union, but he differed with Meany on how to confront them. This was partly a heritage of the split between the AFL and the CIO before the merger. A number of CIO unions had been under the control of communists, so the CIO leaders had to live with them until they became an intolerable political liability, whereas they were anathema to the AFL.

Prestige is another factor in the determination of foreign policy. Unions like to have the word "international" in their titles. Labor leaders enjoy contact with prominent people at meetings and conferences abroad. They like going to Geneva for a month of International Labour Organization (ILO) meetings, or to European capitals for conferences of the International Confederation of Free Trade Unions (ICFTU). There is also some patronage involved. For example, labor attaches at U.S. embassies have often been appointed on recommendation of union presidents, and this has also been true of the staffs of the labor institutes in foreign countries.

Of course there are individuals who hold a firm belief that unions should have a voice in making American foreign policy, and regard themselves as having a unique role to play because of their contact with labor leaders in other countries, some of whom may have been cabinet members or even prime ministers. The AFL, and then the AFL-CIO, have enjoyed close relationships with the British Trades Union Congress, which played a major policy role when the Labour Party was in power in Britain. Fraternal delegates from a number of countries are regularly invited to address AFL-CIO conventions, and the favor is returned.

Finally, there can be direct economic returns to membership in the trade secretariats, international bodies organized on the basis of industry. For example, unions in the steel or construction industries meet periodically to discuss mutual problems, to exchange technological information, and to work out mutually acceptable accommodations.

THE ICFTU

This organization was established in 1949 when it became clear that its predecessor, the World Federation of Trade Unions (WFTU), a product of wartime East-West cooperation, had fallen under the domination of the Soviet Union and its Eastern European satellites. The AFL-CIO contributed a substantial proportion of its budget. There was always some tension between the AFL-CIO leadership and the ICFTU that has been attributed to differences between American and European labor in leadership styles, in relations with communist trade unions, and with respect to the best approach to the promotion of trade unions in developing countries.[1]

There were signs of mutual irritation as early as 1965. The AFL-CIO complained about the lack of Americans on the ICFTU staff. Its financial control officer, an American, had been discharged and the AFL-CIO demanded that he receive a pension. The ICFTU solidarity fund, which was established to help unions in trouble, remained unspent, and Meany demanded—and got—the return of over $800,000. The AFL-CIO, with its 13 million members, had just two seats on the executive board of the ICFTU, the same number as the Canadian Labor Congress, with one million members.

For their part, the European trade unions alleged that the AFL-CIO was out to dominate the ICFTU. The German labor federation expressed the view that the AFL-CIO was too anticommunist, to which the latter retorted that it was inappropriate for one member to criticize another. Meany observed that some European union leaders were on the payrolls of political parties or governments, which impaired their independence of action in pursuing the interests of their members.[2]

What brought the conflict to a head was the application of the Automobile Workers Union for membership in the ICFTU after it had withdrawn from the AFL-CIO. This would have required a positive vote of three-fourths of the ICFTU executive board, which the AFL-CIO and its allies could have blocked. However, the ICFTU congress could have overruled the board and its secretary-general urged Meany not to oppose UAW admission to save himself potential embarrassment.

Nothing could have been designed better to invite a heated reply from the AFL-CIO. Vice-president Joseph Beirne urged immediate withdrawal from the ICFTU. He remarked that the AFL-CIO was being constantly embarrassed by frequent contacts between European and Asian labor leaders with the communists. The Executive Council resolved that it would take no part in any ICFTU activities until assurance was given that it was not proper for the ICFTU or any of its representatives to deal with a dual organization that was hostile to the AFL-CIO—that is, the Auto Workers.[3]

The AFL-CIO wanted the ICFTU to condemn the UAW for its alliance with the Teamsters Union, and when this was not forthcoming, the Executive Council voted to withdraw, with Jacob Potofsky and David Dubinsky not voting. Meany summed up the views of the rest of the Council by asserting that the AFL-CIO had been treated shabbily; that the ICFTU no longer served a useful purpose; that some of its affiliates had sent delegations to the Soviet Union seeking rapprochement; and that the secretary-general had solicited independent UAW membership even before it left the AFL-CIO.[4] A subsequent communication from the ICFTU asking the AFL-CIO to reconsider its decision was rejected, with the advice that the ICFTU refrain from interfering with the internal affairs of its affiliates. The schism continued for more than a decade. In 1980, under new leadership, the Council noted that it had been working in cooperation with the ICFTU, and, in January 1981, appointed a committee to consider the possibility of reaffiliation. A delegation of fifteen AFL-CIO leaders attended a conference that year at which 136 trade unions from seventy-nine countries were represented. Supported by the AFL-CIO, a new secretary-general was elected.

The AFL-CIO hosted ICFTU conferences in 1985 and 1987. The first developed an anti-apartheid policy, while the second focused on the contemporary debt crisis and its impact on developing countries. The AFL-CIO has also maintained close contact with European trade unions through the trade union advisory committee of the Organization for Economic Cooperation and Development and through bilateral meetings with national trade union centers. Lane Kirkland led the AFL-CIO delegation to the 15th World Congress of the ICFTU in 1992. All traces of the earlier animosity seem to have disappeared.

VIETNAM

At the outset of the war in Vietnam the American labor movement was united in support of the U.S. action, but some dissent developed as the years went by, as in the country in general. The conservative, strongly anticommunist wing, including most of the former AFL unions, remained loyal to the Johnson-Nixon policy to the end, while the liberals became increasingly critical. However, the firm support of the war by a substantial majority of unions was never in doubt.

Antiwar resolutions introduced at biennial conventions of the AFL-CIO never got far.

The first debate took place at the 1965 AFL-CIO convention when a resolution in support of the war was introduced. Emil Mazey of the UAW stood up to say that he was "sick with the vulgar display of intolerance that some delegations showed to some college students following Secretary [Dean] Rusk's remarks here the other day," and added that serious blunders had been made and that a settlement of the war should be negotiated. Reuther supported the resolution but rejected a U.S. pullout, adding that full moral responsibility rested with the communists. Meany had declared earlier that

the American trade union movement will use whatever influence it has to see to it that the American people understand what is at stake in the present actions of our government in Southeast Asia, and that sooner or later, the aggressors will realize there is no victory for them by force of arms.[5]

There was more dissent at the 1967 convention, even though the UAW was not in attendance. A resolution was introduced in which "the AFL-CIO reaffirms its unequivocal support of President Johnson's policy in Vietnam." President Charles Cogan of the Teachers Union (AFT) offered a substitute resolution to the effect that the AFL-CIO would take no position on Vietnam, arguing that there was a serious division in labor's ranks that could not be disregarded. He was backed by Leon Davis of the Retail Workers and others. After a long debate, the substitute was defeated and the original resolution adopted.[6] The Executive Council, in its report to the convention, had reiterated its firm conviction that the war was "a Communist war of conquest and part of the Communist drive to dominate the world," and supported the bombing of strategic targets.[7]

The debate continued; two years later the central resolution again favored government policy. There was some sentiment for a major reduction in U.S. military presence, but Meany argued that this would not bring about an honorable peace. The president of the South Vietnam Federation of Labor had visited the Executive Council and was assured of AFL-CIO support in helping secure American assistance for civilian needs. The 1979 convention noted that "although the Nixon administration is systematically winding down the war in Vietnam, Hanoi, with all out support by Moscow and Peking, continues its annexationist drive against all Indochina." The resumption of bombing led the Australian maritime union to boycott American ships, whereupon the U.S. Longshoremen refused to unload Australian ships and the boycott was called off.

When a peace agreement was finally reached the Council welcomed the cessation of hostilities, and declared that the U.S. had emerged with unimpaired credibility as a world power that protected peace and freedom. Loyal to the end, the Council concluded that "in this light, the AFL-CIO has correctly and steadfastly supported the basic Vietnam policy of three administrations."[8]

What is somewhat surprising about the role of the AFL-CIO during Vietnam is not that there was some internal dissension, but how little there was in light of the fierce controversy raging in the country. The chief architect of union policy was George Meany, supported by a solid phalanx of the older unions, the building trades in particular. Had the Auto Workers remained in the Federation they might have led an opposition, but as it was, the liberal wing was leaderless and ineffective.

An interesting contretemps occurred in late 1974 when Meany, asked whether he had been right all along, conceded that he had sometimes been wrong. At a later press conference he said that Richard Nixon and Henrry Kissinger, and perhaps Johnson, had deceived him about the bombing of civilians. But he differentiated himself from the war opponents who wanted Hanoi to win, and insisted that his position was and continued to be the guarantee of self-determination to South Vietnam.[9]

THE INTERNATIONAL LABOUR ORGANIZATION (ILO)

The ILO was formed in 1919 as part of the Treaty of Versailles. The U.S. did not join until 1934, partly because the AFL feared that the organization would be dominated by radical European unions. When the U.S. went in, the American labor delegates were nominated annually by the AFL. With the merger, a unified American labor movement could represent worker interests at the annual conferences in Geneva and in various ILO bodies. The Soviet Union also joined in 1934 but remained inactive until 1954.

One of the problems that soon arose stemmed from the tripartite structure of the ILO. Unlike other international agencies, workers and employers as well as governments served as part of the control mechanisms. Western employers objected that Soviet managers were not independent of their government, as they were supposed to be, and the Western unions, with the AFL-CIO in the lead, denounced Soviet trade unions as puppets. The Russians, for their part, insisted that all their delegates be treated as fully accredited representatives.

The first few years after the merger were relatively quiet ones on this issue. The AFL-CIO Council issued a statement in 1956 "officially reiterating our full and unqualified support of the ILO and of United States membership and active participation therein." It even called for an increase in the U.S. annual financial contribution to the ILO from 1.75 million to three million dollars. The first skirmish occurred when the Council objected to an ILO report on the trade union situation in the USSR, which the Council branded a misleading, Soviet-inspired document. A resolution condemning it was adopted, with Curran, Carey, Dubinsky, and Reuther voting in the minority. After the flurry surrounding the withdrawal of Rudy Faupl, the head of the U.S. labor delegation, the real controversy began to take shape over the Russian demand that as the second largest contributor to the ILO budget, they were entitled to an assistant director generalship, one of the top posts in the organization.

David A. Morse, an American, who became director-general in 1946, was under continuous pressure from both sides. He resigned in 1970 after warning that the Russians could not be denied their claim much longer.

The U.S. backed Wilfred Jenks of Great Britain as his successor on what the AFL-CIO believed was an implied promise that the Russians would not get their wish. A month after assuming office, Jenks informed the U.S that he was appointing a Russian to the post.

The reaction was immediate. Meany told a committee of the House of Representatives that the appointment was the last straw "because whatever this man gets departmental-wise in the ILO he will have hundreds of employees under his supervision . . . he will use that position to make each and every employee a Communist agent whether he wants to be or not." He was seconded by the chief employer delegate, who joined with Meany in the view that they could not get much support from Western Europe.[10]

Congress had no difficulty in deciding to withhold the next appropriation. There was no one to object. The only real constituency the ILO had in the United States was the AFL-CIO, and there only among the leadership. The State Department, however, was firmly opposed to withdrawal. Several events served to mollify the AFL-CIO, including defeat of a Soviet candidate for the chairmanship of the Governing Body, the second most important post in the ILO. Meany was surely not disturbed by a personal attack made by the losing candidate:

Yesterday we heard Mr. Seidman, an envoy of the reactionary leadership of the AFL-CIO, headed by the well known George Meany, who pathologically hates and fears socialism. We know that neither Mr. Seidman nor his chief reflects the views and convictions of the American workers and are merely mouthpieces for major American capitalism and monopoly.[11]

In 1975 The Palestine Liberation Organization was given observer status at the ILO conference. The podium was supposed to be limited to matters within the jurisdictional charter of the ILO, but there were political attacks against the U.S. and Israel in particular without intervention by the chairman. The AFL-CIO convention held that year adopted a resolution strongly condemning the ILO for departing from its original purposes and for permitting erosion of tripartism, calling upon the government to reassess ILO membership. The Executive Council went further; it urged the U.S. Government to give the two-year notice of withdrawal required by the ILO constitution.

The State Department made strenuous efforts to prevent this action. Pope Paul VI made formal representations to President Jimmy Carter as well as a personal appeal to Meany in favor of continued U.S. membership. The Council of the European Community took similar action. A cabinet-level meeting of the Departments of Labor and Commerce on October 12, 1977, which was also attended by representatives of the Chamber of Commerce and the AFL-CIO, adopted a resolution to withdraw. The State Department and National Security

Agency proposed a one-year delay, but membership was terminated on November 1.

The ILO lost a quarter of its budget, though this was made good in part by extra donations from other countries. Progress was made to satisfy the objections of the AFL-CIO, which reported in 1979 that the U.S. strategy was having a positive effect. After the fanfare that preceded withdrawal in 1977, reaffiliation in 1980 was anticlimactic. There was virtually no public discussion of the issues involved. The AFL-CIO proclaimed its satisfaction with ILO movement back to its original practices and purposes. But the Chamber of Commerce disagreed. It had nominated the chief employer delegate in the past, but refused to continue to do so.

A few years later the Executive Council praised the ILO for its work in promoting technical assistance to developing countries. It even filed a complaint with the ILO alleging that public sector employees in the U.S. were being deprived of full collective bargaining rights. The ILO's committee on freedom of association issued findings favorable to the AFL-CIO, but the impact was moral rather than legal since the ILO has no means of enforcing its judgments.

LABOR INSTITUTES

The AFL-CIO has set up and operated a number of institutes designed primarily to assist noncommunist trade unions in developing countries. The nature of the assistance depends on the local situation in each country: the extent of organization, employer attitudes, and, above all, governmental permissiveness. Assistance varies from the provision of educational facilities for union officials and financial help in publishing materials to outright cash grants and anything else that seems useful. This is a major AFL-CIO enterprise.

The first such institute to be established was the American Institute for Free Labor Development (AIFLD) begun in 1962 to operate in Latin America. It was the source of controversy a few years later when it was charged by Victor Reuther, among others, of being a tool of the CIA, a charge that was hotly denied by the AFL-CIO.[12] It receives support from the U.S. Agency for International Development (AID), as do other Federation institutes operating abroad, and also from from the National Endowment for Democracy.

Between 1962 and 1993, more than 750,000 Latin-American trade unionists participated in AIFLD's educational programs. Most of the training, primarily in techniques of organization, has been done abroad, although some union leaders are brought to the United States. Instruction is given in courses that last from one day to several weeks. AIFLD has also made loans to foreign unions for housing, health clinics, water supply, and agricultural development. It works closely with the Inter-American Regional Organization of Workers (ORIT), an arm of the ICFTU.

There has been some criticism of AIFLD's activities in Central America. A more or less neutral resolution at the 1985 AFL-CIO convention involving Nicaragua was denounced by Jerry Brown, secretary-treasurer of the Hospital Workers, who argued that the lessons of Vietnam had not been learned; that the AFL-CIO should speak out against any involvement in the civil war raging in Nicaragua; and that the U.S. should refrain from assisting the Contras. Several speakers seconded him, including Ed Asner of the Screen Actors Guild. Albert Shanker of the Teachers Union defended the resolution, which denounced the Sandinistas, and Kirkland joined him.[13] There had been a similar hedge with respect to the coup in Chile. The 1975 convention had adopted a resolution which stated that "free trade unions did not mourn the departure of a Marxist regime in Chile which brought that nation to political, social, and economic ruin. But free trade unionists cannot condone the autocratic actions of this militaristic, aggressive ruler."[14]

Given the nature of Latin-American politics, AIFLD has had to steer a precarious course between the Left and the Right. Its basic policy has been to work with unions as long as they are not dominated by communists or military dictators. There was justification for the following summary by the Executive Council in 1993:

AIFLD is proud of its over 30 years of successfully promoting the values of democracy to assist Latin-American trade unions to creatively apply their hard-won democratic skills to meet these new challenges and ensure that democratic market economies work for all people.[15]

AFRICAN-AMERICAN LABOR CENTER (AALC)

Established in 1964, this organization is devoted to strengthening African labor movements. It has a staff of 19 in Washington and ten representatives based in eight African field offices. It has sponsored trips for about 150 African union leaders to the U.S. each year, and has worked for the end of apartheid in South Africa.

The problem faced by the AALC, as with other groups seeking to assist African workers, is that there has not been much to work with. Several countries had promising and relatively strong trade unions when they became independent, Ghana, Kenya, and Nigeria among them. Most have fallen under government domination if indeed they have survived at all. With democracy at a low ebb in Africa, AALC has done what it could to keep the spark of unionism alive through educational programs. This has been a much less fruitful arena for AFL-CIO operation than Latin America, where the unions have tended to be a more important part of the political and economic structure.

THE ASIAN-AMERICAN FREE LABOR INSTITUTE (AAFLI)

This institute was established in 1968 with the same agenda as the AIFLD and AALC. It has been very active. About 600,000 Asian trade unionists have participated in its programs over the years. Its principal theaters of operation have been the Philippines, Thailand, Malaysia, and Korea. It assisted in the revival of unionism in the Philippines after the departure of Ferdinand Marcos; it protected the Thai unions from what might have been their extinction by military governments; and it helped sustain the unions in Malaysia in troubled times.

AAFLI has not found a welcome in the three giants of the area: India, Indonesia, and China. The military leaders of Indonesia look upon trade unions as potentially subversive organizations. India's political stance has hindered cooperation. In China, of course, what there is of a labor movement bears no resemblance to democratic forms. The AFL-CIO has maintained a consistently hostile attitude toward China. Kirkland favored withdrawal of the U.S. ambassador, rejection of the Chinese request to join GATT, and a suspension of all sales involving science and technology. He recommended to President Clinton that its most favored nation status be terminated until it improved its human rights. When this was not done, the AFL-CIO called the failure to take action a disappointing setback for those in China fighting for greater democracy.

FREE TRADE UNION INSTITUTE (FTUI)

The FTUI was originally created to help the new democratic unions of Spain and Portugal, but its activities have shifted to the former communist states of Eastern Europe. What with the breakup of the old government-controlled unions and the difficulties of privatization, the unions in these countries have gone different ways.

The earlier FTUI programs were designed to assist Solidarnost in Poland, and this remains a top priority. Contact has also been established with trade unions in the Czech Republic, Slovakia, and Hungary. The situation in Rumania and Bulgaria is still too fluid to warrant substantial relationships. Independent unions in Russia, Belarus, and the Ukraine are having a hard time organizing in the face of opposition from the former communist unions, which are still entrenched in large enterprises.

In Russia, the FTIU has sponsored seminars, financed a union newspaper and a radio network in four cities, set up a foundation for labor research and education, and sent in experienced organizers from Poland. Sorting out the chaotic labor situation in Russia will require far larger resources than the AFL-CIO commands, but it is going about the task with the same enthusiasm that characterized its previous opposition to any contact with Soviet trade unions. If any evidence is needed that the world has really changed, one can point to the fact that the AFL-CIO is willing and able to maintain a presence in Russia.

NOTES

1. John P. Windmuller, "International Unionism in Eclipse: the ICFTU After Two Decades," *Industrial and Labor Relations Review* (July 1970), p. 510.

2. AFL-CIO, *Minutes of the Executive Council*, May 19–20 and September 20–23, 1965.

3. Ibid., December 16, 1968.

4. Ibid., February 17–24, 1969.

5. AFL-CIO, *Proceedings of the Sixth Constitutional Convention*, 1965, pp. 30, 560.

6. AFL-CIO, *Proceedings of the Seventh Constitutional Convention*, 1967, pp. 266 ff.

7. AFL-CIO, *Report of the Executive Council to the Eighth Constitutional Convention*, 1969, p. 92.

8. AFL-CIO, *Report of the Executive Council to the Tenth Constitutional Convention*, 1973, p. 130.

9. Archie Robinson, *George Meany and His Times* (New York; Simon and Schuster, 1981), pp. 341–342.

10. Walter Galenson, *The International Labor Organization* (Madison: University of Wisconsin Press, 1981), p. 115.

11. Ibid., p. 120.

12. For details of these allegations see Sidney Lens, "Lovestone's Diplomacy," *The Nation*, July 6, 1965; Don Kurzman, "Lovestone's Cold War," *The New Republic*, June 25, 1966.

13. AFL-CIO, *Proceedings of the Sixteenth Constitutional Convention*, 1985, p. 17.

14. AFL-CIO, *Proceedings of the Eleventh Constitutional Convention*, 1975, p. 235.

15. AFL-CIO, *Report of the Executive Council to the Nineteenth Constitutional Convention*, 1993, p. 285.

CHAPTER 15

Foreign Trade and Investment

The foreign trade and investment policies of the United States and the countries with which it trades are of immediate and critical importance to union members who are employed in enterprises that are in competition with overseas firms, either in domestic or foreign markets. Their wages and opportunities for employment are at stake. The imposition or removal of a tariff or quota can have severe repercussions.

Where goods or services are imported, the livelihood of working people and the existence of their unions can be threatened. Unions heavily impacted by imports have watched their membership dwindle and have been forced to merge with other organizations. They and the employers with whom they deal are likely to try to preserve their markets by protectionist measures. Unions in export industries are more likely to favor free trade.

The importance of foreign trade to the American economy has grown rapidly. In 1960, the combined total of exports and imports was 9.4 percent of the gross domestic product. It reached 21.7 percent in 1993. To some unions for which foreign trade was not of great importance at the time of the merger, it had become a major concern two decades later. Among them were some of the largest unions in the country, including those in the steel, automobile, and electrical manufacturing industries. There were of course unions not affected by changes in foreign trade patterns, among them the building trades and the services that produced for the domestic market. As a consequence, the AFL-CIO has not always been able to take a unified stand on foreign trade policy. The employees of companies producing aircraft were the beneficiaries of unfettered overseas markets, while the auto workers had their eyes fixed on the domestic market and their share of it.

Economists are almost unanimous in their belief of the benefits of free trade.

It is easy to show by application of the theory of comparative advantages that both parties to trade gain from it. It is not so easy for the trade unionist. It may be true that a job lost to imports will be compensated for by one gained through exports, or even overcompensated. But it is not the same job. Even if the jobs lost are gained in manufacturing, they are not likely to be in the same industry. Given the present structure of industry and the pattern of union organization, the lost job may very well be a union one, while that gained may be nonunion. For the losing union foreign trade is a disaster. For the labor movement as a whole it may lead to a steady loss of members. The author recalls discussing this matter with the head of a national union when in response to the theoretical advantages of trade, he said, "How would you like it if we imported some cheap foreign professors?"

The AFL-CIO came out for the Reciprocal Trade Program in 1958. However, it wanted escape clauses for industries that were hard hit, and assistance to displaced workers in the form of supplementary unemployment benefits up to two-thirds of weekly earnings for fifty-two weeks, retirement at age 60 with full Social Security benefits, retraining, and transportation subsidies to facilitate job search. When it became clear no such assistance would be forthcoming, the Federation nevertheless favored approval of the program on the ground that forty-five million American jobs depended on foreign trade.[1] This is as near as the AFL-CIO ever came to a free trade position.

The first major change in U.S. trade policy with which the AFL-CIO had to deal came in 1962 in the Kennedy Trade Expansion Act. The President was given broad authority over a five-year period to negotiate tariff reductions in exchange for reciprocal action by other countries. Rates could be reduced up to 50 percent but could not be entirely removed for specific products.

The AFL-CIO conditioned its support of the measure on assistance to workers displaced by imports. The Tariff Commission was charged with the duty of determining if there were injury to firms or workers in an industry and initiating benefits, including payments equal to 65 percent of an individual's average weekly wage or 65 percent of the average manufacturing wage, whichever was less; relocation allowances; and extended benefits during retraining. The hope and expectation was that these benefits would enable displaced workers to find other jobs in a reasonable period of time.

The initial experience was not favorable. Three unions were denied relief when it was found that their difficulties were not due to imports. The 1963 AFL-CIO convention adopted a resolution which stated that "labor's support was based on adequate assistance or relief for those adversely affected by imports. The continued support for liberal trade depends on the fulfillment of this premise."[2] Low unemployment for the rest of the decade and a more liberal administration of the Trade Adjustment Assistance Act, which contained the assistance program, appeared to satisfy the labor movement.

When unemployment began to rise in the 1970s foreign trade was more carefully scrutinized by the AFL-CIO. The Exective Council urged the necessity of new legislative, administrative, and negotiating policies to prevent further erosion of American production, market disruption, and the export of U.S. jobs. It opposed low tariffs for less-developed countries. It also advocated giving the President power to prohibit the export of American capital, a theme that was to become more insistent.[3]

In 1975 the Council undertook a thorough review of the foreign trade situation and came up with extensive recommendations for policy changes. Among them were the following:

1. The Trade Act of 1974 (which the AFL-CIO had not opposed) gave the President authority to curb imports that were affecting employment adversely and contributing to a trade deficit. He was urged to use this authority liberally.

2. The President should curb the export of raw materials, technology, and products that adversely affect the national interest.

3. Congress should examine carefully all trade agreements that might affect jobs and industries.

4. The Overseas Private Investment Corporation, a government agency set up to encourage investment abroad, should be terminated.[4]

These and other recommendations indicate how far the AFL-CIO had departed from its earlier free trade position. From then on, the Federation became a force for protection as the ravages of rising imports became more obvious.

When the Carter administration came into office the dollar value of exports rose but was not directly translated into employment gains because of the capital-intensive nature of agriculture, a major export. In 1976, the U.S. adopted the General System of Preferences that removed tariffs on imports from almost all developing nations, where they were being produced with cheap labor. Foreign investment in the U.S. took the form largely of acquisition of going concerns rather than new ventures. There were special tariff allowances for foreign assembly work contracted out by American firms and then reimported.

Adjustment assistance became the major issue as far as the unions were concerned. Between April 1975 and July 1977, 2,234 petitions for relief had been filed. They represented 530,000 workers, but only 230,000 were certified. Almost every American industry was affected, one way or another. The assistance program was not a panacea. The trade stance of the AFL-CIO changed dramatically. The report of the 1977 convention states:

The AFL-CIO supports healthy, fair trade that will build a strong American economy. We oppose the continued export of American jobs and industry, which has undermined the economy. We shall pursue every possible relief for the injury already sustained, as well as new legislation to halt the drain on this nation's economy.[5]

In subsequent biennial reviews of developments in foreign trade, the Council reiterated the complaints and occasionally approved a change. In 1979, for example, it referred to the favorable effect of the trigger price mechanism on the import of steel from Japan and Europe. Quotas were imposed on the import of Chinese textiles. A labor-management coalition achieved a curb on Japanese color television sets. In the three and one-half years from 1977 to 1979, 440,000 workers received adjustment benefits, though denials continued to be greater than certifications. When the Trade Agreement Act of 1979 was being debated by Congress, the Federation complained that since the Act had to be voted up or down without change, it was unable to present amendments that it favored.[6]

While the Federation had been critical of many trade policies adopted by the Carter administration, the volume and sharpness of its complaints rose with the advent of Ronald Reagan. Legislation was introduced in 1981 to limit the import of automobiles, but it was made moot by a voluntary quota accepted by Japan. Import quotas on shoes from Taiwan and Korea were lifted. The head of the Food and Commercial Workers Union said that his organization had lost two-hundred footwear companies and 75,000 jobs to imports. The AFL-CIO opposed the extension of most favored nation treatment to China, but to no avail.[7]

The most bitter protest was against the reduction of benefits to displaced workers. The 1982 budget cut funding by 77 percent. Until October 1, 1981, benefits equaled 70 percent of lost wages up to the average factory wage. Thereafter, compensation was limited to the unemployment compensation level in each state, which was considerably lower.

New AFL-CIO recommendations for job protection emerged as time went on. One involved the the enactment of domestic content laws by which foreign companies with access to U.S. markets would be required to produce a portion of parts and components in the U.S. Emphasis was placed on the necessity of protecting services as well as goods and preventing access of such imports if corresponding exports were barred. This referred to banking, broadcasting, construction, entertainment, and air transport, all of which had encountered export barriers.[8]

Government trade policies were castigated. The report of the 1985 conventions states:

While other nations are maintaining or increasing their barriers to imports, subsidizing their exports, and directing investment flows to benefit their own economies, the Reagan Administration clings to a belief in 'free trade' and mythical market forces. At a time when positive government action is desperately needed to reverse the erosion of America's industrial base, this rejection of reality has had disastrous consequences for the U.S. economy.

A voluntary restraint agreement on automobiles expired in 1984, but was extended for a year with increased quotas. Foreshadowing a controversy in the making, the 1985 report states:

Congress should carefully review any future bilateral free trade agreements to assure that domestic production will be enhanced. We are especially concerned about possible developments along these lines with respect to the neighboring countries of Canada and Mexico. Simple trade liberalization will not benefit American industry and workers.[9]

Several government actions served to exacerbate the controversy. A recommendation by the International Trade Commission to put quotas on shoes retailing for more than five dollars a pair was rejected. The Senate voted to set quotas on the import of textiles in the face of a veto threat by the White House, which was eventually forthcoming. The Trade Adjustment Assistance Act was extended for six years, but the suggestion of a tax on imports to finance the program was dropped, and benefits were limited to workers who had exhausted unemployment compensation.

Several attempts by Congress to legislate trade reform in the direction of protection were also vetoed. By a vote of 295–115, the House passed a bill in 1986 supported by the AFL-CIO that called for a 10 percent reduction in trade deficits as well as measures against discriminatory practices by foreign countries. It defined as ''unreasonable'' trade practices denial of collective bargaining rights, child labor, and poor health and labor standards, any of which would be subject to retaliation. The Senate did not act on it because of administration opposition. A modified version was enacted by the House a year later by a close margin but failed in the Senate.

The next attempt came in April 1988, when the Senate passed a bill mandating retaliation against any action that violated agreements or involved unjustifiable trade practices, which included internationally accepted worker rights. The House passed a similar bill, but it received the inevitable veto. The House overrode the veto, but the Senate failed to do so by three votes. The culmination of this legislative campaign came in August 1988, with the enactment of the Omnibus Trade and Competitiveness Act, less than three months before a presidential election. It provided for greater congressional oversight and defined denial of internationally recognized worker rights as an unfair trade practice. This was a political bow to the unions.

Complaints by individual unions continued to mount. The UAW charged that the voluntary restraint agreement with Japan was poorly enforced and did not cover auto parts. William Bywater (Electrical Workers) stated that membership in his union had fallen from 350,000 to 100,000 in ten years because of imports from Japan. Lynn Williams (Steelworkers) noted that some of the countries sending steel to the United States had no mills of their own. Morton Bahr (Communications Workers) said that his industry had been heavily penetrated by foreign firms.

An event that presaged the great trade battle of the 1990s was the inauguration of the U.S.-Canada Free Trade Agreement on January 1, 1989. To the American unions this agreement, ''which will largely benefit multinational corporations, does not establish reciprocal trading regimes, and fails to provide necessary protections for workers on either side of the border.'' With respect to ongoing negotiations with Mexico, ''problems relating to the growth of the Maquiladora program and its impact on U.S. industry are not being addressed.''[10] A resolution adopted at the 1989 convention cited the fact that Mexican wages were below those in Korea, Taiwan, Brazil, and Singapore, and expressed concern that free trade with Mexico was bound to move American jobs there.

The Bush trade policy was no more to the liking of the unions than Reagan's had been. An act to give some protection to textiles, apparel, and footwear was vetoed. Of eleven countries cited by the AFL-CIO as not being eligible for tariff privileges because workers' rights were denied, only Liberia and Sudan were penalized. The AFL-CIO filed suit in a federal court to force the government to conduct careful investigations of the others, as the law required. The 1991 AFL-CIO convention adopted the longest foreign trade resolution in its history, calling for reduction of automobile imports, stabilization of the textile, apparel, and shoe industries, further limitation of steel imports, maintenance of the domestic electronics and television industries, domestic processing of American raw materials, and the continued prohibition of the export of Alaskan oil. It also demanded that exports of American technology be banned, that the capital flow be regulated, and that an international agreement to improve labor standards be negotiated. There were many other items on this menu, all in the direction of protection.

THE NORTH AMERICAN FREE TRADE AGREEMENT (NAFTA)

The controversy over this agreement absorbed more of the attention and resources of the AFL-CIO than had any previous piece of trade legislation. In June 1990, Presidents Bush and Carlos Salinas de Gortari of Mexico announced their intention to begin negotiations on an agreement, and Canada joined in. The AFL-CIO asserted that for such an agreement to be successful, all of the following elements would have to be included, among others.

1. The right to organize and bargain collectively, strong workplace health and safety standards, appropriate minimum wages, and the elimination of child labor.
2. A reduction in wage differentials among the three countries.
3. Funds for the enforcement of environmental laws along the borders.
4. Denial of trade benefits to countries that transferred production to Mexico in order to gain access to U.S. and Canadian markets.
5. Improvement of border infrastructure, including sewers, water, electricity, and housing.
6. Additional debt relief to Mexico to enable it to invest at home and improve living standards.
7. Tough rules of origin, so that other countries could not transship goods through Mexico and Canada.
8. A decent trade adjustment assistance program.[11]

Clinton had promised during his election campaign that he would oppose any U.S.-Mexican trade agreement that did not include work standards and environmental protection, but that he would not reopen the agreement that had been reached by Bush. The unions believed that there would be adequate safeguards in side agreements, but they soon discovered that there was no effective enforcement machinery.

The side agreement on labor rights and standards actually represents a weakening of existing remedies available under U.S. law. It fails to identify even minimal labor rights and standards to be enforced, establishes an oversight process so vague, discretionary, and protracted that a timely resolution to a dispute would be virtually impossible.

There was a great gulf between what the AFL-CIO had specified as a condition of its support of NAFTA and the final draft of the treaty. The unions were convinced that it would lead to the loss of half a million American jobs and downward pressure on American wages. The Council decided on an all-out fight against ratification. Richard Gephardt, the House majority leader, called for major revisions. Marches and rallies were organized in various parts of the country.

What the unions had not counted on was the depth of Clinton's commitment to see the treaty through. Initial soundings in Congress indicated that he would not have enough votes to prevail. He called many wavering congressmen to the White House, made promises of quid pro quo in exchange for their votes, and even said that he would defend Republicans if they were challenged on NAFTA in the next elections. The result was a 234–200 affirmative vote in the House and 61–38 in the Senate. "Labor was stunned by the extraordinary spectacle of a Democratic president allied with a two-thirds majority of Republicans, vigorously horse trading to gain enough Democratic votes to pass a trade agreement negotiated by his Republican predecessor. Lane Kirkland fumed: ''The President has clearly abdicated his role as the leader of the Democratic Party. His position is contrary to that of the majority of his own party in the Congress.''[12]

The GATT treaty was an anticlimax. The unions had urged its rejection because of inadequate provision for workers' rights, the lack of sufficient protection of import-sensitive industries, and the inability of the U.S. to fight restrictive measures imposed around the world. As stated at the 1993 convention:

While commerce today is indeed global, social protection and regulation—factors that are necessary to humanize the market and to help promote a more equitable distribution of its benefits—remain the responsibility of national governments. This conflict needs to be resolved if trade is to expand and benefit the greatest number of people.[13]

The final outcome was the same; GATT was approved.

Thus ended the saga of American labor and foreign trade. It is a story of frustration, small at first, then growing to large dimensions. The central focus was persistent belief of the unions that free trade would inevitably lead to a loss of American employment and union jobs in particular. Events have borne them out. Industries were destroyed or decimated, and union membership suffered.

Trade adjustment assistance did not prove to be a palliative. Funds appropriated for retraining and mobility were scarcely used. State employment offices had neither the staffs nor the experience necessary to administer these portions of the law, and the ambitious program of converting skills ended up as standard unemployment compensation at best.

The problem for the unions was that they were swimming against a strong free trade tide and did not have the political power to turn it. There is a firm belief among Americans that trade protection is inimical to economic growth and prosperity, which was abetted by the fact that until fairly recently, foreign trade was not a major factor in the American economy.

The question now, in the light of large trade imbalances and the restrictive practices adopted by some of America's principal trading partners—Japan in particular—is whether the position of the labor movement on foreign trade is without some merit.

NOTES

1. *AFL-CIO News*, June 7, 1956.

2. AFL-CIO, *Proceedings of the Fifth Constitutional Convention*, 1963, p. 268.

3. AFL-CIO, *Report of the Executive Council to the Ninth Constitutional Convention*, 1971, p. 127.

4. AFL-CIO, *Report of the Executive Council to the Eleventh Constitutional Convention*, 1975, pp. 142–147.

5. AFL-CIO, *Report of the Executive Council to the Twelfth Constitutional Convention*, 1977, pp. 108–115.

6. AFL-CIO, *Report of the Executive Council to the Thirteenth Constitutional Convention*, 1979, pp. 92–99.

7. AFL-CIO, *Report of the Executive Council to the Fourteenth Constitutional Convention*, 1981, pp. 234–236.

8. AFL-CIO, *Report of the Executive Council to the Fifteenth Constitutional Convention*, 1983, pp. 98–104.

9. AFL-CIO, *Report of the Executive Council to the Sixteenth Constitutional Convention*, 1985, pp. 154–165.

10. AFL-CIO, *Report of the Executive Council to the Eighteenth Constitutional Convention*, 1989, pp. 157–166.

11. AFL-CIO, *Report of the Executive Council to the Nineteenth Constitutional Convention*, 1991, p. 170.

12. *AFL-CIO News*, November 29, 1993.

13. AFL-CIO, *Report of the Executive Council to the Twentieth Constitutional Convention*, 1993, p. 169.

CHAPTER 16

Six National Unions

A history of the labor movement should include an account of the national unions affiliated with the AFL-CIO. There are some ninety-five of these at the present writing, and covering even a large number of them would be a daunting task. What this chapter does instead is to consider developments in six AFL-CIO unions that among them furnish the Federation with 42 percent of its membership. Not all of them have been success stories. Some have lost members and others have grown since the merger. The reasons for this disparate experience provide a clue to the fortunes of the labor movement as a whole. It was possible to organize large numbers of workers when there were unfriendly governments and intense employer opposition. On the other hand, some powerful unions were not able to arrest their own decline.

AUTOMOBILE, AEROSPACE, AND AGRICULTURAL IMPLEMENT WORKERS (UAW)

This union had 1,260,000 members at the time of the merger. Data for subsequent years appear in Table 16-1. It is difficult to determine density ratios since membership is not coterminous with industry employment statistics. In 1977 about half its members worked outside the basic automobile industry. Measured against the labor force of the big three auto producers—GM, Ford, and Chrysler—the density was very high and continued so throughout the postmerger period, since these firms remained almost completely organized.

The years between the merger and the withdrawal of the UAW from the AFL-CIO were good ones for the union. The hourly labor cost for a GM worker rose by 68 percent compared with 36 percent for manufacturing as a whole. Mem-

Table 16.1
Membership in the United Automobile Workers and the Steelworkers Unions, 1955–1993 (thousands of persons)

Year	Auto Workers	Steelworkers
1955	1,260	980
1959	1,060	892
1963	1,033	805
1967	1,325	952
1971	1,500 (1972)[a]	950
1975	1,400 (1977)[a]	1,062
1979	na	964
1983	1,010	707
1987	998	494
1991	840	459
1993	771	421

Sources: AFL-CIO, *Reports of the Executive Councils to the Biennial Conventions*; United Automobile Workers, *Report of President Woodcock to the 1972 and 1977 Conventions.*[a]

bership increased by 100,000. The Japanese invasion of the U.S. automobile market was still in its infancy.

Differences over wages and other conditions were settled through collective bargaining. The union usually selected one of the big three as an initial target when contracts had to be renewed, and when an agreement was reached, attempted to impose its terms on the others. There was a breakthrough in 1961 when a GM agreement increased the supplementary unemployment benefits which the union had pioneered to 75 percent of an employee's take-home pay and raised the duration from 26 to 52 weeks. Full hospital and other medical costs were granted, and pensions were increased. Ford took a strike of 120,000 before going along with the GM agreement.

It was Chrysler's turn in 1964, when the union secured additional benefits—early retirement, life insurance, and higher pensions for retired workers. There was a 31-day strike against GM over noneconomic issues that eventually yielded the union a satisfactory agreement. Ford was the initial target in 1967, and it took a month-long strike for the union to win a new benefit—a guaranteed annual wage that gave workers with seven years of seniority a guarantee of 85 percent of their wages for up to a year. The union agreed to an annual cap on cost of living allowances of eight cents an hour, which proved costly in subsequent inflation years.

The UAW had the reputation of being a very liberal union, as evidenced by some of its actions. It set up a public review board in 1957, consisting of seven outsiders, to hear appeals from members who charged that the union had violated their rights. The complainants were entitled to counsel and on occasion the board reversed decisions of the union's executive board or its conventions. A decade later, Walter Reuther introduced a resolution at the 1965 AFL-CIO convention calling for "a public program which will replace our fragmented, costly, inefficient, and inadequate arrangements for health care with an acceptable nationwide program for comprehensive, high quality health service which is accessible to all Americans."[1] This was almost thirty years before the Clinton campaign for a national health program.

The tragic death of Walter Reuther in 1970 and the succession of Leonard Woodcock to the presidency did little to change the manner in which the UAW operated. The UAW continued its upward march throughout the inflation and recession of the 1970's, and in 1970 felt confident enough to take on GM as its initial target, the first time since 1945. A strike of two months proved necessary before agreement could be reached.

Negotiations during the rest of the decade took place amid rapidly rising prices and the start of foreign competition. Earnings of production workers in transportation equipment, dominated by the automobile industry, rose a bit more than consumer prices. The firms began to tighten up. In 1976, for example, GM demanded substantial cuts in benefits. Automation was beginning to take its toll. An interesting footnote to the period's events was a meeting of the UAW and a Soviet metalworkers' delegation. It had to be held in Canada because visas for the U.S. were denied. The UAW noted, "We have repeatedly protested this highly discriminatory policy of refusing visas to communist trade unionists, but so far to no avail."[2] Needless to say, George Meany was a staunch proponent of this policy.

The 1980s were years of crisis for the UAW, as for most of the labor movement. They were ushered in by the near bankruptcy of Chrysler in 1979. At a time when 300,000 auto workers had been laid off, the demise of Chrysler would have been a disaster. The corporation and the union in tandem managed to convince the federal administration that the only way out was a government loan guarantee. The U.S. Treasury estimated that if Chrysler had failed, the cost to taxpayers would have been $3 billion in welfare costs, lost revenue, and unemployment compensation.

For its part, the UAW gave Chrysler a concession in labor costs, mandated by Congress as part of the arrangement. In return, Douglas Fraser, who had succeeded Woodcock as UAW president, was made a member of the Chrysler board of directors. He promised to speak for the workers at every opportunity and to abstain and leave the room if an issue involved a conflict of interest.

Next came the problem of automobile imports from Japan. The Japanese sent almost two million passenger cars to the U.S. in 1980, rising to 2.5 million by 1985, then falling slowly to 1.9 million by 1990. The union petitioned the International Trade Commission for import restrictions; the Japanese companies agreed to accept a quota of 1.6 million cars a year. The UAW had its first confrontation with a new Japanese-owned plant in the U.S., the Kawasaki motorcycle plant in Lincoln, Nebraska. "The report of the 1980 convention stated: "It is simply outrageous that Japanese companies which operate unionized plants in Japan will engage in wholesale violation of U.S. labor laws and slander of unions like the UAW."[3] The company had told its employees that the UAW was a promoter of violence, greed, and corruption.

Negotiations from 1980 to 1983 centered on job security. In an agreement with Ford, the union made concessions that were the equivalent of two weeks of paid vacation a year and that set limits on annual wage increases. In return, Ford promised to share profits and not to close plants for two years because of shifting work to outside suppliers. A similar agreement was reached with GM. The union began to spread its wings by annexing District 65 of the Distributive Workers Union, the remnant of an old CIO union which had a membership mainly of white-collar workers. But efforts to organize new Honda and Nissan auto plants failed.

During the next three years, the UAW once more concentrated on job security. It was able to negotiate a program under which no worker with at least a year's seniority could be laid off due to outsourcing, new technology, or negotiated productivity increases. Workers whose positions were eliminated went into a job bank where they drew their regular pay checks while training for other jobs, or while performing other assignments. A Chrysler agreement brought parity with Ford and GM; the company had earned $2.3 billion in 1984 and it agreed to an immediate payment of $2,100 to each employee in partial compensation for the deficits of the below-pattern years. Owen Bieber succeeded Fraser as president and replaced him on the Chrysler board.

In an attempt to compete with the Japanese in the production of low-cost small cars, GM decided to build a plant in Tennessee for a new car, the Saturn. The company entered into an unusual agreement with the UAW while the plant was still in the construction stage. There was to be no distinction among personnel, including management, in parking or cafeteria facilities. UAW members were to receive salaries rather than weekly wages and could be laid off only under catastrophic circumstances. The union would have full access to the books of the plant. In return, the union agreed to simplify the structure of job classification: one for production workers and three for skills. The base rates were to be 80 percent of those at other GM plants, plus additional compensation depending on performance, product quality, and profits.

Many AFL-CIO affiliates have local unions in Canada. A number of them have faced separatist movements among the locals. Several factors may have led to this development: the greater militancy of some Canadian workers, differences in economic and political conditions on the two sides of the border, and a growing nationalism in Canada. The union most affected in terms of membership has been the UAW. The basic problem appears to have been differences in economic circumstances and their effects on collective bargaining. These became conspicuous in the Chrysler debacle.

The Canadian locals went along when the union was obliged to make concessions under the terms of the loan guarantee, but when Chrysler asked for an additional concession soon thereafter, the Canadian workers refused to reopen the contract. It was their view that production costs were already lower in Canada than in the U.S. due to currency exchange rates and the lower cost of benefits because of Canadian government welfare programs. Subsequent contract reopenings led in 1982 to a five-week strike in Canada that was settled when Chrysler gave the Canadian workers a wage increase.

This set the stage for reopening the Ford and GM contracts before they expired in 1982. At this time, 55,000 of 180,000 hourly workers at Ford and 150,000 of 340,000 at GM were on layoff. The UAW again made concessions. The Canadians refused to discuss the contracts prior to their expiration dates, and since there was less unemployment among their members, they felt they could get better terms. In fact, they did.

The climax came in the 1984 GM negotiations, when the recession was over and profits high. The UAW traded wage concessions for increased employment security. The Canadians followed a different strategy; they went for a wage increase, more paid vacation time, and a new income security program. Despite pressure from Owen Bieber to comply with the UAW pattern, they refused, backed their refusal by a strike, and got their way in the end.

Bieber told the 1986 UAW convention what happened next. Bob White, the head of the Canadian department of the UAW, moved at a meeting of the UAW executive board that Canadian workers be given autonomy, including the right to issue strike authorizations. The board turned this down by a vote of 24–1, whereupon White introduced a second motion calling for a completely independent auto union for Canada, which carried 17–7, and in September 1985, the split was consummated.[4] The Canadian group took with it 140,000 members, about 10 percent of total UAW membership.

Concessions were over by 1987, although the emphasis was still on unemployment. The heart of the Ford agreement, the first to be signed, was a provision for guaranteed employment numbers, by which Ford was required to maintain specified levels of employment in each Ford-UAW unit for the first three years of the contract, backed by $500 million in funding. There could be no layoffs for any reason except carefully defined reductions in the volume of production linked to market conditions, or because of power failures. When a person with less than one year's seniority reached one year, the guarantee was to be increased by one. There was to be a reduction when an employee died, quit, or retired. Wages were raised by 3 percent and cost of living allowances, which had been suspended, were reinstated. GM and Chrysler dutifully followed this pattern.

The companies were warned that employee cooperation in raising productivity was contingent on four principles:

1. Workers would need to be assured of a long-term future of secure employment and their participation in any plans that might lead to the elimination of jobs.

2. All new forms of work would be subject to joint agreement.

3. Workplace democracy would have to be real democracy. Management could not just pretend to listen.

4. Changes in the workplace were to be matched by changes in the front office.[5]

The concept of employee participation in management was vigorously debated at the 1989 convention. An opposition group called New Directions, of which Victor Reuther was a prominent member, submitted a resolution condemning membership on company boards by union officials. Fraser was charged with giving legitimacy to plant closings when he was on the Chrysler board, and of having compromised the bargaining process. It was alleged that the "team concept" merely meant cutthroat competition among locals. A spokesman for the union administration termed it naive to give up positions of power, and pointed out that Fraser and Bieber had modified corporate policy to the advantage of the union.

How can you serve two masters, asked the dissidents? What has board membership done for Chrysler workers? Are not economic democracy schemes merely a coverup for harsher management dictatorship? Bieber said in rebuttal that he had spoken and voted against high management salaries, and added: "It is a lonely, lonely place at the Chrysler board of having one vote out of 18, but it is the only voice on that Chrysler board that puts forth the argument of the workers, no one else there does it." After a long and bitter debate that covered the issues thoroughly, the minority resolution was defeated.[6]

Almost one-third of the workers organized by the UAW between 1986 and 1989 were technicians, office employees, or professionals. The union was making progress in the public and service sectors rather than in manufacturing. Several new councils had been added to the union structure to accommodate the new members: academic, health care, and the public sector. District 65 was raised to the status of a department, with 50,000 members, including 5,000 legal employees, 700 professionals in publishing, 1,000 day care workers, 1,700 academic employees, and 5,000 research assistants. The UAW was on the way to becoming a general union.

The year 1990 marked the first time in over a decade that there was simultaneous bargaining with all three companies, although GM was the initial target. All the agreements that were reached limited layoffs stemming from volume reductions to thirty-six weeks. Workers had to be recalled when this limit was reached, and if no jobs were available, they were placed in a job opportunity bank with the first call on vacancies. The union was given greater input into outsourcing decisions.

Japan became a matter of top concern. In the three years to 1992, Japanese automobile manufacturers doubled their plant capacity in the United States, in addition to setting up component plants. The latter maintained close connections with Japanese suppliers, so that the domestic content of Japanese cars assembled in the United States was low. The UAW cited as an example a Honda plant in Ohio, one of twelve "transplants" operating in the United States, with an annual output of 400,000 cars. Half the parts it used were imported, and of parts sourced in the United States, more than three-fifths came from transplanted suppliers. Moreover, the parts produced in the United States tended to be of low value, mainly hardware and trim. The transplants had a competitive advantage not only because they were newer but also because they received tax abatements from the states in which they were located, as well as state-financed infrastructure. Their benefit costs were also lower because their labor force was younger.

The objections would have been less vehement if the United States had been able to organize the transplants. Half of them were located in right-to-work states. By way of contrast, the UAW sent a representative to Germany to get the support of the works council of Mercedes-Benz in their drive to organize a new German plant in North Carolina. They also received support from the Swedish Metalworkers Union in a Volvo-GM truck strike, and from French unions in a Renault truck plant. The UAW did maintain contact with the Japanese auto union, but that was an organization with virtually no power.

Master contracts negotiated in 1993 gave promise of labor peace for the next three years, but GM became embroiled with local issues, which had to be negotiated separately. There were many local strikes over productivity, overtime, outsourcing, and job security. Local unions were less willing to let the national union bargain for them on local issues they regarded as critical. For example, GM was required to add ninety-two jobs at a Shreveport, Louisiana plant to improve cooling and ventilation systems, and to require subcontractors to hire GM workers who had been laid off and who earlier had been producing the same parts as the workers employed by the subcontractor.

Membership in the UAW in 1993 was 40 percent less than the level at the time of the merger. It was not the victim of the antiunion wave that swept the country during the 1980s and even earlier. Its hegemony was unchallenged by the major automobile producers. Its decline was due basically to technological change and to Japanese inroads into the American automobile industry. When Japanese imports of passenger cars had captured a quarter of the U.S. market and encountered barriers to further progress, Japanese firms began moving production into the country. They did not have to deal with independent unions in Japan, and for the most part followed what might be called a company-union policy in the U.S. The UAW will eventually organize them, but the ravages of advancing technology will still be there. The UAW can only regain its former status in the labor movement by bringing in more diverse groups of service employees than it has already done.

THE UNITED STEELWORKERS OF AMERICA (USW)

The membership data for the Steelworkers Union (Table 16.1) reveal a rising trend to the mid-1970s, then a precipitous decline during the following decade.

By 1993 the union was down to 43 percent of its merger membership, a much more severe drop than that of the UAW. The USW was a major victim of industrial restructuring and foreign competition.

The first post-merger convention of the USW came soon after it had won a favorable contract with the steel companies following a four-month strike, including a modified union shop, which the union had long sought. The leaders had proposed that the office of a national director for Canada be eliminated, but the convention voted down the proposal by a large majority. The Canadians wanted a share of the leadership, a portent of things to come. There was opposition to an increase in dues from $3.00 to $5.00 a month, but in the end it was accepted.

It required a strike of 116 days to reach a new contract in 1960. Twelve weeks after the strike had begun, President Dwight Eisenhower intervened, and when he was unable to bring about a settlement, a Taft-Hartley injunction was secured on the ground that the national health and safety were endangered. There were no major gains in the end, and a fall in steel production led to the layoff of 150,000 workers.

At the urging of President Kennedy, negotiations for a new contract began early in 1962. This time there was no strike and both wages and other conditions were improved. Kennedy believed that he had an understanding with the steel companies that there would be no price increases, but prices were nonetheless raised. After a good deal of pressure by the administration, including a number of presidential pronouncements, they were virtually forced to rescind the increases.

Opposition within the USW to the presidency of David McDonald had been rising, in part because of the mediocre performance of the union. The 1964 convention marked the first serious challenge to his leadership, when I.W. Abel, the secretary-treasurer, threw his hat in the ring. After a long campaign Abel won by a small margin, the first time the head of a major AFL-CIO union was ousted by an internal revolt.[7]

Another round of collective bargaining began soon after Abel was installed. President Lyndon Johnson used the full power and prestige of the White House to prevent a strike, citing the needs of the war in Vietnam. The workers received a generous wage increase. The settlement was marred when a few months later, R. Conrad Cooper, the chief negotiator for the steel companies, launched a bitter attack on the union in general and Abel in particular, and lauded the deposed McDonald as "an example of true labor statesmanship," a characterization that puzzled many. It may have been that Abel was closer to the Reuther line on social policy than McDonald had been. Indeed, one of the highlights of the 1955 USW convention, chaired by Abel, was the very friendly reception he received when he spoke there. McDonald and Reuther were never friends, a factor in bringing about the merger in 1955.

The USW absorbed the Mine, Mill, and Smelter Workers Union in 1967, a union that had been expelled from the CIO because of its communist leadership.

This brought in 25,000 members in the U.S. and 15,000 in Canada. But it also involved the USW in a long strike against the ferrous metals industry that lasted eight months and embraced 50,000 workers. The AFL-CIO and its affiliates contributed $800,000 in support of the strike. A settlement was eventually reached with the intervention of the federal administration. The USW spent more and got less than it normally secured in the steel industry.

The 1968 negotiations in basic steel produced an agreement without a strike. Behind it was the beginning of a company strategy that was to transform collective bargaining in the industry. This involved the stockpiling of steel products in anticipation of the contract termination date. If a strike occurred, customers were assured that their supplies would not be cut off. If there were no strike, the inventories could be drawn down by curtailing operations and laying workers off. In either event, the workers and the union suffered. Once again, at the close of negotiations, the companies raised steel prices for which they were denounced by President Johnson, who threatened to cut off their access to defense contracts. Prices were reduced.

The 1970s were good years for the USW on the whole. It absorbed several unions in addition to Mine Mill—the Stoneworkers with 11,000 members, and District 50, an organization that John L. Lewis had set up in an effort to expand the United Mine Workers into a general union. By 1971 it had signed up 170,000 members in chemicals, construction, mining, and utilities. These acquisitions helped sustain USW membership, for employment in basic steel was falling. In 1955, the ratio of salaried to production employment in steel was 16.9 percent, and by 1971 it had grown to 24.7 percent. Steel imports were beginning to hurt, though the industry received some protection through voluntary import restraint agreements with the major exporters of steel products to the U.S.

As an aftermath to the 1971 negotiations the USW and the steel companies entered into what was termed the experimental negotiating agreement (ENA), which represented a revolutionary change in steel collective bargaining. Bonuses were given for savings by the elimination of stockpiling. There was to be two-tiered bargaining; it was to start on February 1 on the national level, and if an agreement could not be reached either party could submit unresolved issues to an impartial arbitration panel for final decision. There was a separate right to strike on local issues. This meant compulsory arbitration on matters that had led to work stoppages in the past.

The 1974 negotiations went according to plan, and it looked as though a corner had been turned in the industry's industrial relations. Despite the fact that the economic situation of the industry began to deteriorate, the 1977 negotiations continued according to ENA, and the USW received the best total wage and benefit package ever. Abel was succeeded by Lloyd McBride in a contested election that was appealed to the Labor Department and upheld there. The year 1980 was the last good one for the union. The ENA procedure was continued, but significantly, it was not renewed. By 1982, more than 100,000 union members in basic steel were out of work, since foreign steel had captured a quarter of the U.S. market. McBride termed the economic atmosphere the greatest threat to collective bargaining since the days of Calvin Coolidge and Herbert Hoover.

Worse was yet to come. In addition to the 100,000 members who were out permanently, 170,000 were on layoff. Almost every company was closing plants, including the largest producer, USX. The negotiations in 1983 took place in a distressed industry. Concessions became the order of the day. Wages were reduced, as well as premium pay for Sunday work, and cost of living allowances were suspended. The companies committed themselves to use labor cost savings to improve production facilities. Canadian nationalism, which had caused a split in the UAW, was mitigated by the election of Lynn Williams, a Canadian, to fill the unexpired term of McBride, who died in 1983.

The USW attempted to compensate for membership loss by organizing outside the industry. It reported in 1984 that it had in its ranks 28,000 office employees, 20,000 shipyard workers, 7,000 hospital employees, 1,000 mushroom miners, 600 bank employees, 200 butchers, and 900 bakers. The USW convention urged expansion of the union's jurisdiction to "any unorganized workers anywhere in the Western hemisphere." But the USW was far behind the UAW in converting itself into a general union.

Production of steel in the United States reached a low point in 1986. By that time some 200,000 steel workers had been permanently displaced, compensated only in part by the takeover of 34,000 members of the Upholsterers Union. Industry-wide bargaining, the pattern since the war, was replaced by bargaining company by company. A strike against Wheeling Steel in 1985 was the first against a major company in fifteen years. Wheeling went into bankruptcy and the court allowed it to install a large cut in wages and benefits. The union demanded and secured replacement of top management officials, and a new agreement restored much of the cut and gave the union a seat on the company's board of directors. This was followed a year later by an agreement with another bankrupt firm, LTV Steel, under which the union received some company stock, and with National Steel, where wages were reduced and company stock was given to the workers in return.

The culmination of the breakdown of the collective bargaining system that had been crafted over the years came in 1986 when USX locked out 22,000 workers after having rejected a union offer to keep working during negotiations for a new contract. After a six-month shutdown the union accepted a reduction in wages and other benefits in return for a commitment to reduce outsourcing. The impact of all these events are clear from the membership data in Table 16.1, a loss of 470,000 members in eight years.

Things improved somewhat in the 1990s as the industry began to dig its way out of the recession. Bethlehem steel set a pattern in 1990 by which the union won substantial gains, which was followed by five of the seven major steel companies. Perhaps the most interesting development of this period was the union's adoption of the principle of worker participation in management. A task force on freedom and democracy, in a report to the 1990 convention, cited the German and Swedish experience, and concluded:

The conduct of an enterprise is much too important a matter to be left in the hands of corporate managers. Their record in both our countries [the U.S. and Canada] is marred by mistakes for which workers shouldered the loss. . . . So far, the response of the Steel-workers to our experimental worker participation programs has been overwhelmingly positive. It will remain so provided the union is a fully powered participant in every stage of the process.[8]

By 1992, the union was heavily involved in participation programs. Members were majority stockholders in seventeen enterprises and minority stockholders in twelve. Most of them were small and had been taken over when they were experiencing financial difficulties. One of the most far-reaching arrangements was at Inland Steel, whose operations were not unlike the German codetermi-nation model. The agreement provided for union nomination of a corporate board member and established three partnership committees:

1. The joint strategic partnership committee to function at the board level and oversee matters concerning technological change, staffing, productivity, safety and health is-sues, and plant utilization.
2. The joint leadership committees, charged with the operational performance of indi-vidual plants in the areas of cost and quality performance.
3. The joint leadership committees, consisting of elected union representatives and man-agement representatives at the departmental level.

Industrial relations improved in 1994, perhaps because of a union-friendly administration in Washington. USX signed a five-year contract under which workers received a $5,000 bonus over the life of the contract, plus additional amounts depending on profits. There were to be no layoffs except for the usual disasters. And continuing the worker participation trend, the USW was to receive a 20 percent equity in a new steel company formed from plants of Bethlehem Steel that had been shut down. The company was named BRW Steel and the union was entitled to two board seats. To avoid involvement with the National Labor Relations Board (NLRB), union recognition would be granted on the basis of card checks. One additional development that was new for the USW; George Becker was elected president without opposition to replace Lynn Williams, who retired.

The Steelworkers Union faces an uncertain future. In the course of forty years it was transformed from a giant into a medium-sized organization. Of all the initially large unions in the AFL-CIO, it is the principal victim of industrial restructuring. After the debacle of the 1980s, it succeeded in reestablishing itself as a major player in the steel industry. What happens next depends largely on the fate of that industry.

Table 16.2
Membership in Three AFL-CIO Unions, 1955–1993 (thousands of persons)

Year	State, County, and Municipal Employees	Service Employees	Food and Commercial Workers
1955	99	205	—
1959	173	—	—
1963	212	305 (1965)	—
1967	297	352 (1969)	—
1971	458	396	—
1975	647	480	—
1979	889	528	1,076
1983	959	589	993
1987	1,032	762	1,000
1991	1,191	881	997
1993	1,167	919	997

Source: AFL-CIO, *Reports of the Executive Councils to the Biennial Conventions.*

AMERICAN FEDERATION OF STATE, COUNTY, AND MUNICIPAL EMPLOYEES (AFSCME)

This was a relatively small union at the time of the merger. By 1993 it had well over a million members (Table 16-2). This was in part a function of the tremendous growth of state and municipal employment; in 1955, there were 4.7 million people in this category, and by 1993 almost 16 million. These people did not organize themselves. It took an aggressive union to do it.

AFSCME was chartered by the AFL in 1936, with Arnold Zander as founder and president. It grew slowly and spent a good deal of its resources on stimulating the extension of the civil service system. Not until the merger did the union give priority to collective bargaining, union security, and signed agreements. It did not have the protection of federal statutes against unfair labor practices, nor could it seek recognition through NLRB elections. Its concern was with state and local legislation.

There was a good deal of strife in the union's early post-merger history. One of the principal issues was centralization. The district councils, the main organizational echelons below the national union, were largely self-financing and wanted to manage their own affairs. This was particularly true of District Council 37 in New York City whose director, Jerry Wurf, was a young and ambitious leader. He became head of an opposition caucus and defeated Zander for the presidency in 1964.

Another bone of contention was a housing program in which the union was involved. Zander believed that it was part of the union's mission to provide low-cost housing—and not only for union members. Funds for the houses were provided by the Federal Housing Administration, but the union provided letters of credit in the event that federal funds were not sufficient to complete the units. The union not only had to rid itself of a $200,000 liability on this score, but also owed a similar amount to the AFL-CIO for affiliation fees. It cleared its debt by selling its headquarters building in Washington and renting office space. This was hardly the picture of an affluent organization.

The union had about 200,000 members when Wurf became president, twice the number at the time of the merger. He undertook a national organizing campaign, with assistance from the AFL-CIO and the UAW. There were many strikes, usually in disregard of no-strike statutes, such as one in Ohio that shut down four large cities. Perhaps its most important victory was in New York City, which became a focus of AFSCME power. It involved 35,000 hospital employees whom the Teamsters were also trying to organize. Victor Gotbaum, who was later to become the spokesman for the New York labor movement, was brought in from Chicago to run the campaign. An election was held under the auspices of the City, and although the Teamsters were able to delay recognition for nine months, AFSCME eventually became the bargaining agent. It also picked up 7,000 members of an independent Social Service Employees Union after a month-long strike. The became the pattern of AFSCME growth—it came in spurts.

An important change in Wurf's strategy was his willingness to surrender the right of public employees to strike in return for compulsory arbitration. He said in an interview:

I fight bitterly for the right to strike, the *right* to strike. But I don't think there's any principle involved in striking. Striking is a tactic to persuade an employer to deal with us. If it can be avoided, almost any price ought to be paid in order to avoid a strike.[9]

Compulsory arbitration was heresy in AFL-CIO circles, and at one point Meany, who was no admirer of Wurf, castigated him for his views. However, given the nature of the civil service clientele who were the organizational targets of AFSCME, a viable substitute for the strike made sense.

Competition from other unions was a problem that plagued AFSCME, particularly from the Service Employees, the Laborers, and the Communications Workers. The difficulty was to reconcile claims of jurisdiction based on occupation with those covering the public sector. Should a carpenter or plumber employed by a municipality belong to a construction union or AFSCME? In winning the affiliation of the Ohio Civil Service Association in 1983, for example, AFSCME competed with the Communications Workers, the Food Workers, and the building trades. It gained a majority in eight of fourteen bargaining units that included 35,000 of the 42,000 employees eligible to vote. The AFL-CIO regarded these competitive campaigns a waste of union resources but had difficulty preventing them. Wurf wrote of organizational victories in Hawaii, New Jersey, and Washington State, netting 56,000 new members in four months:

We are beating the pants off our opposition, particularly those two private sector unions [the Laborers and Service Employees] that have moved hungrily into our jurisdiction. We are finding at the state and local government levels that public employees want full-time public employee unionism, not part-time private industry outfits dabbling in government unions.[10]

While the AFL-CIO appreciated the affiliation fees paid by AFSCME, relations between the two were not always harmonious. When AFSCME asked the AFL-CIO to set up a public employees department, Meany delayed. Wurf then joined with the independent National Education Association in the formation of a Coalition of Public Employee Associations, later called the Coalition of American Public Employees, as a lobbying organization. Two years later the Fire Fighters Union and the independent National Treasury Employees joined, creating a potentially formidable bloc in opposition to the AFL-CIO. The reply of the AFL-CIO was to form the public employees department that Wurf had demanded, with which 27 AFL-CIO unions eventually affiliated.

AFSCME became embroiled in a controversy with the Carter administration, which had proposed a welfare reform plan providing for the creation of 1.4 million government jobs for welfare recipients. They would be paid the minimum wage, would not receive fringe benefits, and would be laid off for five weeks each year. AFSCME objected strongly to the proposed wage rates as well as to the creation of an underprivileged public labor force. The proposal was not enacted, but it succeeded in cooling any enthusiasm felt by the union for Jimmy Carter's reelection.

AFSCME's greatest coup centered on the New York State Civil Service Employees Association (CSEA), which started as an insurance agency but gradually took on bargaining functions. An independent organization, it faced raiding by a number of AFL-CIO unions. In 1978, it lost the right to represent 45,000 professional and technical employees to a coalition of the Service and Teachers unions. AFSCME offered it a refuge, and a merger was arranged. CSEA was promised two seats on AFSCME's board, and autonomy rather than being put under the jurisdiction of a district council. In this manner AFSCME added 30 percent to its membership.

When Wurf died in 1981, AFSCME claimed more than a million members. This was a phenomenal rate of growth, unmatched since the heyday of CIO expansion in the 1930s. The name of Jerry Wurf is not well known to the general public, but he ranks as one of the most successful labor leaders in the history of the American trade union movement.

Growth continued during the 1980s, though not as rapidly. Gerald W. McEntee succeeded Wurf. A breakdown of AFSCME membership in 1984 revealed the following: There were 415,000 state employees and 355,000 who worked for cities and counties; 105,000 in school districts; and 130,000 in hospitals, universities, and nonprofit institutions. By occupation, 400,000 were in health care, 190,000 were clericals, 110,000 were technicians and professionals, and 100,000 were in law enforcement and corrections. Women constituted 40 percent of membership, and blacks and hispanics 30 percent. It was a very heterogeneous organization. There was some debate at the 1984 convention on an old question: Should people on workfare be organized? It was feared that regular workers would be displaced if they were, but on the other hand, they could be used as strikebreakers if they were not. A resolution favoring organization was defeated.

A resolution at the 1988 convention proposed the elimination of an age limitation of 65 years for national officers standing for election. Some delegates argued that this was essential if leadership vitality were to be maintained, while others called it undemocratic and discriminatory. The bar was retained, but there was a postscript. A federal judge ruled against this provision, and the union decided not to contest it. Another issue involved dues for part-time employees, who were difficult to organize if they were charged full dues. These were people like crossing guards, school bus drivers, and cafeteria employees. A resolution favoring lower dues was defeated because it would have raised havoc with the finances of some locals that consisted largely of part-timers.

The 1990s found AFSCME ensconced as the third largest union in the AFL-CIO. It was fortunate in being able to operate in a sector that was not subjected to the employer offensive. Some of its employers were having a hard time balancing their budgets, but political pressures could force them to improvise. This was particularly true of the larger cities where liberal Democrats often held sway.

Not all AFSCME members are white-collar workers, but enough are to make it clear that with the right messages and tactics, they can be organized as readily as the blue-collar workers who were the trade union pioneers. The same is true of women and minority groups. There are still large numbers of people in occupations corresponding to those in AFSCME, whose unionization could turn around the overall decline of the labor movement.

SERVICE EMPLOYEES INTERNATIONAL UNION (SEIU)

At the time of the merger, the SEIU was the Building Service Employees Union and was sometimes referred to disparagingly as the janitors' union. The word ''building'' was dropped from its title in 1966 on condition that this would not extend its jurisdiction. While it did not abandon its original constituents, the SEIU grew rapidly by going after every eligible service group in sight. The president of the union, John J. Sweeney, boasted later that his union was the most diverse in the AFL-CIO. Like AFSCME, it grew largely by absorbing groups of independent employees. For example, it picked up 100,000 members by taking in the California State Employees Association; 50,000 members of the National Association of Government Employees; and 52,000 members of New York local 1199, which had become a national union of hospital employees. This was not achieved without strenuous activities. It established a 3 percent annual membership growth target in 1988 and gave financial awards to locals that exceeded the target quota. During the previous four years it had grown by 4.4 percent annually.

The SEIU has between seventy and eighty thousand members in Canada, most employed in health care. The difficulty there is that most of these people work in the public sector where there is binding arbitration and limitations on the right to strike. Arbitration decisions are often handed down a year after contract expiration. The Canadian locals have asked for more autonomy, but thus far this has not been granted.

The SEIU does not eschew strikes, at least in the private sector. It mounted a successful strike against Beverly enterprises, the largest chain of nursing homes in the U.S. It created a Justice for Janitors campaign as a militant model. Locals were advised that

strikes (and the threat of strikes) are still among the most powerful weapons available to us as we fight to improve our members' living standards. In the Healthcare, Building Service, and Public Divisions we have seen again and again that strikes which were well planned and well run have enabled us to achieve advances that were unimaginable without the strike and to strengthen the strategic position of the union with the employer for years in the future.[11]

The goals and strategy of the SEIU were set out by its 1992 convention:

Building Service. Expand the Justice for Janitors campaign, strengthen relationships with developers, owners, and contractors.

Health care. End site-by-site nursing home organizing and bargaining, and develop regional bargaining; become the union of home-care workers while the industry is still in its infancy.

Office Workers. Organize around such issues as sexual harassment; expand the use of hotlines.

Industrial and Allied. Organize nonunion stadiums, arenas, convention centers, and racetracks, utilizing the potential leverage offered by public financing.

Public. Recognize that this sector is being restructured by downsizing, privatization, and contracting out; organize the private sector to make these events less attractive.

In 1992 it was determined that 50 percent of SEIU members were female, 20 percent black, and 10 percent Latino. The leadership composition of the larger locals was 25 percent female and 15 percent people of color. The union claims to be the largest in the health care industry with 400,000 members, including

5,000 in Puerto Rico and 52,000 in Canada. Its 150,000 office workers were mainly in the public sector.

The SEIU presents the picture of a confident, well-led union that may well maintain the steady rate of growth that has lifted it to fourth place in the AFL-CIO. Its advice to the AFL-CIO: ''The labor movement cannot continue to spend nearly 95 percent of its resources just to service its existing membership only to act surprised when that membership continues to diminish in size, and therefore, influence.''[12] Its emphasis on organizing lends credence to its claim that ''SEIU is the union best positioned to lead the resurgence of the labor movement.''

UNITED FOOD AND COMMERCIAL WORKERS UNION
(UFW)

This union grew out of a series of mergers. The Packinghouse Workers, a former CIO union, merged with the Butcher Workmen, ex-AFL, in 1968 to form a half a million-member union. The Retail Clerks absorbed the Boot and Shoe Workers in 1977. The two groups joined in 1979 to create a million-member union. Barbers, Hairdressers, and Cosmetologists came in a year later. Several other groups were absorbed subsequently: the Insurance Workers, the United Retail Workers (independent), and the Canadian Brewery Workers, who became an autonomous national organization within the UFW framework.

President William Wynn complained to his 1988 convention about the ''merger mania'' in American industry. Meat packing was particularly affected. A number of old-line companies either went out of business or were reorganized, including Swift, Armour, Cudahy, Wilson, Morrell, Hygrade, and Rath. During the five-year period 1983 to 1988, the UFW had organized 400,000 workers, yet the percentage of organization in its area of operation had not risen. It was in one door and out the other. Its strike fund had been depleted. Elections were avoided wherever possible; the percentage of new members recruited through NLRB elections fell from 25 percent to 8 percent.

There was a leveraged buyout at Safeway, one of the union's largest employers, with 37,000 jobs at stake. Safeway had intended to sell some of its divisions without requiring the new owners to rehire members or recognize the union, but in response to union pressure it agreed to make severance payments to discharged employees in its Dallas division and to seek buyers who would at least negotiate with the union on new contracts. This helped reduce the eventual job loss.

Half a million workers joined the UFW from 1988 to 1993, yet the membership total reported to the AFL-CIO remained almost unchanged. A great deal was spent on organization. Several union packinghouses changed ownership and had to be organized all over again. Since its foundation in 1979, 40 percent of all its funds spent to finance strikes involved packinghouses, yet only 6 percent of its members worked in this industry.

The union also faced what amounted to a restructuring of one of its industries. While more than 80 percent of food dollars were spent in union grocery chains, there was a growing threat from supercenters that sold a mixture of food and nonfood items. Some were very large, involved in marketing clothing, small appliances, auto supplies, and sporting goods, among other items. Wal-Mart and K-Mart, both nonunion, were examples. This meant fewer employers with larger market shares and lower employment. One way of fighting them was for local unions to prepare detailed documents showing their impact on downtown business and prevailing on local communities to deny the necessary zoning permits. There was also some negative impact from French, Belgian, and Dutch retailers who were entering the U.S. market and paying lower wages.

Oddly enough, UFW had some problems with the Steelworkers. When a merger was arranged with the Retail and Wholesale Union in 1993, a group of 19,000 Canadian members withdrew, renamed themselves the Retail and Whole-sale Union of Canada, and were chartered by the Steelworkers Union. UFW locals in Pittsburgh found themselves confronting Steelworkers who were allegedly trying to sign inferior contracts. Wynn remarked that:

the Steelworkers is a great union. It is a great union to steel workers, but it is a lousy union for the building trades, it is a lousy union for the people who work in grocery stores, and it is a lousy union for the people who work in hotels.[13]

Wynn retired in 1994 and was succeeded by Douglas H. Dority.

UFW remained one of the largest unions in the AFL-CIO during the difficult years of the 1980s, but it was not the most dynamic one. Restructuring of retailing and strong opposition from the meat packers meant that it had to run hard to stand in the same place. It has a large potential pool from which to draw new members, but this will not be an easy task.

THE INTERNATIONAL BROTHERHOOD OF TEAMSTERS (IBT)

The membership of the Teamsters at the time of the merger was 1.33 million, based on per capita payments to the AFL-CIO. Reliable subsequent data are hard to come by. Figures occasionally given by union officials are not consistent. Suffice it to say that the figures of 1.379 million in 1991 and 1.316 million in 1993, reported to the AFL-CIO when the union had reaffiliated, make it the largest union in the Federation. Membership probably attained higher levels during the intervening years

A great deal has been written about the Teamsters, most of it focused on the character of its leadership.[14] The incredible thing is that it managed to survive and prosper amid a tremendous barrage of bad publicity and active government intervention. Not only that, the trucking industry was changing in a manner unfavorable to the union. This is a story that deserves much greater space than can be allotted here.

The McClellan Committee described Dave Beck, who presided over the union from 1952 to 1957, as a man who "brought shame and disrepute on the American labor movement. . . . This committee can only conclude that the labor movement is well rid of Dave Beck as it would be well rid of others like him. The public and the 17 million union members in America deserve better."[15] After he stepped down from the Teamster post, Beck served a term in prison for tax evasion and grand larceny.

Beck was succeeded by James R. Hoffa, perhaps the most notorious figure in American labor history. He was president from 1957 to 1967, when he was imprisoned for attempting to bribe a jury in an earlier trial for bribery, obstruction, and conspiracy, in which he was acquitted. His sentence was commuted in 1971 by President Richard Nixon after he served almost five years, with the condition that he could not engage in union business for an additional nine years. Were it not for this constraint he could probably have regained the union presidency. As things turned out, Hoffa disappeared in 1975; there was a widely held presumption that he was murdered by an organized crime group.

The next in line was Frank E. Fitzsimmons, who died in office in 1981. His successor, Roy Williams, ran afoul of the law. He served as president only eighteen months before being convicted of conspiring to bribe a U.S. senator who had a key vote in legislation deregulating trucking company rates. His replacement was Jackie Presser, whose indictment federal authorities sought for embezzlement. He escaped prison, however, by acting as an FBI informant against crime figures. His death in 1988 brought William McCarthy to the presidency.

A consent decree issued by a federal court in 1989 installed court-appointed overseers to look out for Teamster ties to organized crime and to ensure membership referenda in place of convention elections in naming top union officials. The result was the election in 1992 of Ron Carey, the leader of a reform faction within the union. The decree also provided for an independent review board to monitor Teamster affairs. Allegations of misconduct brought by Carey's opponents were subsequently rejected by the board.[16]

Did the quality of Teamster leadership influence collective bargaining and other union activities? The fact is that Hoffa had strong rank and file support because of the economic gains achieved during his tenure. There was a general belief among the members that Hoffa was being victimized unfairly by employers. Moreover, the power of the Teamsters to interfere with deliveries of goods and equipment enabled the union to become the nearest thing to a general union that has existed in the U.S. Untrammeled by jurisdictional constraints, the IBT organized egg farmers, retail clerks, airline stewardesses, furniture makers, office workers, policemen, tree surgeons, and many others.[17] Hoffa's greatest achievement was the negotiation in 1964 of the first industrywide contract in trucking—covering almost half a million workers in both over-the-road and local transportation.

After Hoffa was gone, the number of occupations represented by the union multipled. Zoo keepers, meter maids, university maintenance workers, and turnpike toll employees were added to the list. The Teamsters had a toe-hold in the airline industry as well as in food processing, soft drinks, and beer. They had acquired a reputation for tough bargaining and many diverse groups either sought their protection or had it thrust upon them.

Beginning in the 1970s, the government began efforts to deregulate the trucking industry in the interest of greater competition. Nonunion companies proliferated, as well as truck leasing companies which paid below the union scale. The Motor Carriers Act of 1980, passed over strenuous union opposition, finally brought about deregulation, leading to rate and wage cutting and a rash of bankruptcies.

A small number of dissidents formed the Teamsters for a Democratic Union (TDU) and began to preach reform. At the 1981 Teamster convention they introduced a resolution calling for the establishment of an ethical practices committee modeled on that of the AFL-CIO. The high point of the convention was a speech by a Canadian delegate, Diana Kilmury, declaring:

I didn't say you all were a bunch of crooks. I don't think that, but what I do think is that we've had a few rotten apples before, and if you're too damn scared to have an Ethical Practices Committee that yourselves, the General Executive Board, will control, then by God, you must be up to something.[18]

The resolution failed to be adopted.

Senator Robert Dole addressed the 1986 convention by phone and referred to the Teamsters as the voice of American workers for eighty years. He added: "I applaud the International Brotherhood of Teamsters for its commitment to the American worker and our country."[19] As a means of securing political cover, the Teamsters were almost alone in supporting Republican presidential candidates. Kennedy was denounced as a danger to the nation, and Nixon received Teamster support, which may have helped Hoffa secure an early release from prison. They did support Hubert Humphrey, but until 1992 were consistent in their endorsement of Republicans. McCarthy said of George Bush that "he doesn't forget his friends. . . . He appreciates all of the Teamsters because we played a big part in his election."[20] Finally, in 1992, the Teamsters joined the rest of the labor movement politically, reflecting the victory of the reform forces.

At his first press conference after becoming president, Carey remarked:

I want to welcome all of you to a new Teamster union. The union that's been won back by its members. The union that's going to work for its members. A union that will not be tolerating corruption. . . . What our members have said today is good-bye to the Mafia, good-bye to concessionary contracts. It's good-bye to those who have lined their pockets and put the membership in last place.[21]

He expanded the organizational staff and the budget, but he did not succeed in reducing the role of the government review board, which was chaired by William H. Webster, a former director of the FBI and the CIA.

Fairly early in his administration, Carey called a national trucking strike that lasted 24 days, the longest in the union's history. However, the strike was less crippling to the economy than earlier ones had been, reflecting a decline in Teamster power. Trucking Management, Inc., which had bargained for 300 companies in 1979, represented only twenty-three in 1994. Union members covered under industrywide bargaining fell from 300,000 to 110,000. The agreement finally reached was a mixed blessing for the union, and was ratified after a good deal of criticism of Carey.[22]

The Teamsters Union was weakened in the 1980s by a combination of trucking deregulation and recession. It had claimed over two million members in 1980, but there was no indication of how this figure was derived. Although the number of truckers was rising during the decade, union jobs were falling. The Teamsters were not the victims of the kind of industrial restructuring that took place in the steel and automobile industries, but rather of their inability to stem the growth of the nonunion sector in trucking. They had expanded their jurisdiction to include a variety of other occupations, but truck driving remains the backbone of the union. It is too soon to tell how they will fare under their new leadership.

NOTES

1. AFL-CIO, *Proceedings of the Sixth Constitutional Convention*, 1965, p. 512.

2. United Automobile Workers, *Report of the President to the 1977 Convention*, pp. 124–125.

3. United Automobile Workers, *Report of the President to the 1980 Convention*, p. 56.

4. For a detailed account of this event, see John Holmes and Anthony Rusonik, *The Breakup of an International Union* (Kingston, Canada: Industrial Relations Center, Queens University at Kingston, 1991).

5. United Automobile Workers, *Report of the President to the 1989 Convention*, pp. 13–15.

6. United Automobile Workers, *Proceedings of the 1989 Convention*, pp. 173–183.

7. For an account of this contest, see John Herling, *Right to Challenge* (New York: Harper and Row, 1972), pp. 264–303.

8. United Steelworkers of America, *Proceedings of the 1990 Convention*, pp. 57–58.

9. Joseph C. Goulden, *Labor's Last Angry Man* (New York: Atheneum, 1982), p. 184.

10. Ibid., p. 197.

11. Service Employees International Union, *Official Proceedings of the 1993 Convention*, p. 337.

12. Ibid., pp. 330–331.

13. United Food and Commercial Workers, *Proceedings of the 1993 Convention*, p. 83.

14. Kenneth C. Crowe, *Collision* (New York: Charles Scribner's Sons, 1993); Dan La Botz, *Rank and File Rebellion* (New York: Verso, 1990); Arthur A. Sloane, *Hoffa* (Cambridge, MA: MIT Press, 1991).

15. U.S. Senate, *Interim Report of the Select Committee on Improper Activities in the Labor or Management Field*, 1958, p. 87.

16. *New York Times*, July 12, 1994, p. B2.

17. Sloane, *Hoffa*, p. 181.

18. International Brotherhood of Teamsters, *Proceedings of the 1981 Convention*, p. 286.

19. International Brotherhood of Teamsters, *Proceedings of the 1986 Convention*, p. 44.

20. International Brotherhood of Teamsters, *Proceedings of the 1991 Convention*, p. 29.

21. Crowe, *Collision*, p. 258.

22. *Monthly Labor Review* (January 1985), pp. 24–25.

CHAPTER 17

The Road Ahead

The adversity suffered by the AFL-CIO is part of a general decline of trade unionism in the economically developed areas of the world. The causes of the decline are not uniform, but there are some similarities, including industrial restructuring, expansion of the service industries, and changes in the demographic and occupational structures of the labor force. Union membership has fallen even where governments have been consistently pro-union (Australia, for example) and where employers have recognized the social legitimacy of unions (Germany), suggesting that more fundamental forces are at work.[1]

The fact that the phenomenon of decline is shared by labor organizations elsewhere is no consolation for American labor. At a meeting of the AFL-CIO Executive Council in February 1995, it "engaged in a rare display of self-examination. Battered by defeats from the Administration and Congress, the council recognized more publicly than ever before that the federation is suffering from the same sort of powerlessness that afflicts millions of workers."[2]

This is not to say that the entire American labor movement is in retreat. Some of its affiliates have achieved remarkable membership growth in recent years. John Sweeney, the president of one of them, is among those pressing harder for reform. There was even the suggestion of an old idea, the creation of a Labor Party, to field candidates in national elections. This is not likely to occur, but it reflects the frustration of some Federation leaders.

There is no mystery about where the potential growth points are located. Both statistical data and recent union experience make this clear. Table 17.1 shows the extent of union representation in 1993 by industry. AFSCME may have difficulty in matching its past growth because of already high density and the legislative situation in states that are largely nonunion. The Food and Commercial Workers and the Service Employees, on the other hand, have an enormous

Table 17.1

Employment and Union Membership by Industry, 1993 (thousands of people)

Industry	Employment	Percent union members	Percent represented by unions
Mining	643	16.0	17.6
Construction	4,638	20.0	21.0
Manufacturing	18,710	19.2	20.3
Transport and public utilities	6,313	30.5	32.5
Wholesale and retail trade	21,655	6.3	6.9
Finance, insurance, real estate	6,783	1.9	2.6
Services	26,235	5.8	7.0
Government	18,616	37.7	43.6

Source: Statistical Abstract of the United States, 1994, p. 439.

potential for further growth. There is still room for expansion in manufacturing and construction, but the number of jobs in the former is unlikely to increase, while the construcion unions will have to recapture the home-building labor market, where they are not protected by the Davis-Bacon Act.

The projected employment growth rates for the coming decade suggest that computer and data processing, health care, and automobile repairing stand out. Several unions have already entered the health field and it is too much to expect that a single health services union might replace the established jurisdictions, even though this might promote unionization. More mergers might help; there have been 133 since the AFL and the CIO joined forces. "Mergers enable unions to enhance bargaining and organizing power, achieve economies of scale, eliminate costly duplication of efforts, and increase administrative and financial resources."[3]

Progress may depend on the extent to which unions are willing to commit their resources to organizing. The great drives that began in 1936 and were financed largely by the substantial treasury of the United Mine Workers are unlikely to be repeated. The then-somnolent AFL was forced to reply by putting on campaigns of its own. During the last four months of 1936, the AFL payroll for organizers amounted to $82,000. The corresponding figure for 1937 was $466,000. The number of salaried organizers on its payroll rose from 35 in 1937 to 232 in 1938.

The AFL-CIO recently rejected a proposal to set up a national strike fund to help unions in financial difficulty becouse it would have involved a large increase in the per capita affiliation fee. Administrative costs take a large portion of union expenditures, and there is an understandable reluctance to divert large sums to national campaigns with uncertain yields. As for the issues that might appeal to target groups, higher wages and shorter hours are always attractive, but the unions are faced with severe economic constraints in many industries, particularly those that are subject to foreign competition. Job security has become a major concern, as some unions have stressed—UAW agreements constituting a good example.

The remarkable increase in the female labor force participation rate is another important variable. Women already constitute a large proportion of membership in some unions, particularly those that have achieved high rates of growth. They are still not organized in proportion to their labor force participation. Some unions have made a real effort to accommodate their needs, but policies such as suspicion of part-time work, which many women desire at some stage of their careers, can be counterproductive. Sponsorship of child care facilities rather than leaving them to employers to initiate may help bring more women into unions.

The Union Privilege Program of the AFL-CIO was established in 1986 as an organizing device, and the claim has been made that it has achieved its purpose of retaining old members and attracting new ones. The problem with this approach is that most of the benefits are readily available in the market—mortgages, credit cards, a motor club, life insurance, bank loans, and legal services. A glance at newspapers and junk mail shows the intensity of competition for these consumer services. The Program is a selling point, but whether it is a significant factor in the decision to join a union is open to question. On the other hand, the presence of union representatives on corporate boards and in policy-making at the factory level may turn out to be an attractive feature, as it has in a number of European countries.

How much does the future of American trade unionism depend on favorable legislative action? There is little doubt that banning permanent replacements in a strike situation would increase the readiness of workers to engage in work stoppages. Speeding up the NLRB election procedure along the lines recommended by the Commission on Worker-Management Relations would undoubtedly be of great help in organizing campaigns, as would implementing its ideas about facilitating the first contract.

The attainment of favorable legislation depends on the success of political action. The efforts of COPE and other groups have not yielded much in the way of returns in recent years. The last time the unions made a major contribution to the election of a president was in the Kennedy-Johnson era, when their numbers and political power were at a higher level. The benefits derived from their support of Carter, and thus far from Clinton, have not been great. Part of their problem is an internal one. In the 1994 Congressional elections, union households voted 61 to 39 percent for Democratic candidates, somewhat below the more usual 63 to 37 percent split. Mario Cuomo, who treated the unions well in New York as governor, received only 51 percent of the union vote in his campaign for reelection. If 80 or 85 percent of union members could be persuaded to vote for candidates endorsed by their unions, there would be a difference, for unions are among the largest organized groups in the country.

It is possible that organizations outside the AFL-CIO will align themselves with it if their economic interests converge. For example, the American Medical Association might become a quasi-union if a national health scheme is adopted. The same might be true of associations of engineers, scientists, university professors, and others. Political cooperation with the National Education Association would add a great deal to union clout. How to persuade their own members, let alone outside groups, to unite on critical policies is a formidable task, but one that the unions will have to undertake to make political action more profitable.

During the years between World War I and the Great Depression, the labor movement was battered and almost moribund. Then came the tremendous explosion of the New Deal and the advice of President Roosevelt to the 1944 Democratic convention to "clear with Sidney" the choice of a vice-presidential candidate. The American labor movement, despite its subsequent decline, still has a great deal of vitality. The AFL-CIO has more than 13 million members, and there are another three and a half million in independent unions and associations that resemble unions. To achieve the legitimacy enjoyed by trade unions in a dozen foreign countries will not be an easy task for the American labor movement, but neither is it an impossible one.

NOTES

1. Walter Galenson, *Trade Union Growth and Decline: An International Study* (Westport, Conn.: Praeger, 1994).
2. *New York Times*, February 26, 1995, p. 23.
3. *Monthly Labor Review* (February 1995), p. 24.

Postscript

Two major events in the AFL-CIO story occurred after the manuscript for this book had been completed. The first concerns the succession to the presidency of the organization. Lane Kirkland decided not to seek reelection at the 1995 convention and in the ordinary course of events, his successor would be Thomas R. Donohue, the long-time secretary-treasurer. However, John J. Sweeney, the president of the Service Employees Union, announced that he would contest the election.

Sweeney, who is backed by some of the largest unions in the Federation, argued that the Kirkland-Donohue leadership has not been sufficiently aggressive in seeking to organize new members and has failed to give sufficient recognition to women and minorities in its top positions. To give his colleague an advantage in the election, Kirkland resigned in August and Donohue was appointed to succeed him on an interim basis by the Executive Council. Donohue committed himself to a sharp increase in the organizing budget of the AFL-CIO to train 1,500 new organizers. At the same time, Barbara Easterling, vice-president of the Communications Workers, was designated to succeed Donohue as AFL-CIO secretary treasurer. Under its constitution, the principal officers of the AFL-CIO are elected for terms of two years at its biennial conventions.

The second major development came in the form of an announcement by three large national unions—the Auto Workers, the Steel Workers, and the Machinists—that they were planning to merge over the next few years. The combined membership of the three unions was 1,666,000 in 1993, and the consolidated union would be the largest in the AFL-CIO. All had suffered substantial membership losses over the last decade, and hoped that they could turn

their situations around by enhancing their resources and avoiding costly competitive organizing campaigns.

Both of these events marked a new chapter in AFL-CIO history. It will be
some time before it is clear whether they are sufficient to arrest the declining
fortunes of the American labor movement.

Bibliography

Addison, John T. and McKensey Blackburn. "The Worker Adjustment and Retraining Notification Act." *Industrial and Labor Relations Review*, vol. 47, no. 4 (1994).

AFL-CIO, *Minutes of the Meetings of the Executive Council*, 1955–1969.

AFL-CIO, *Proceedings of the Biennial Conventions*, 1955–1993.

AFL-CIO, *Reports of the Executive Council to the Biennial Conventions*, 1955–1993.

AFL-CIO News, 1955–1995, various issues.

Chaison, George N. and Dileep G. Dhavala. "A Note on the Severity of the Decline in Union Organizing Activity." *Industrial and Labor Relations Review* (April 1990).

Chamot, Dennis. "Scientists and Unions: the New Reality." *American Federationist* (September 1974).

Cole, David T. "The Internal Disputes Plan is a Working Reality." *American Federationist* (June 1969).

Commission on the Future of Worker-Management Relations, *Report and Recommendations*. Washington, DC: Government Printing Office, 1994.

Cooke, William N. "The Rising Toll of Discrimination Against Union Activities." *Industrial Relations* (Fall 1985).

Crain, Marion, "Gender and Union Organizing." *Industrial and Labor Relations Review* (January 1984).

Crowe, Kenneth C. *Collision*. New York: Charles Scribner's Sons, 1993.

Ellwood, Daniel T. and Glen Fine. "The Impact of Right to Work Laws on Union Organizing." *Journal of Political Economy*, vol. 95, no. 2 (1987).

Feuille, Peter. "Unionism in the Public Sector." *Journal of Labor Research* (Fall 1991).

Freeman, Richard B. and Casey Ichniowski. *When Public Sector Workers Organize.* Chicago: University of Chicago Press, 1988.

Freeman, Richard B. and James L. Medoff. *What Do Unions Do?* New York: Basic Books, 1984.

Galenson, Walter, *The International Labor Organization.* Madison: University of Wisconsin Press, 1981.

————. *Trade Union Growth and Decline.* Westport, CT: Praeger, 1994.

Gould, William B., IV. *A Primer in American Labor Law.* 3d ed. Cambridge, Mass.: MIT Press, 1993.

Goulden, Joseph C. *Labor's Last Angry Man.* New York: Atheneum, 1982.

Herling, John. *Right to Challenge.* New York: Harper and Row, 1972.

Hurd, Richard W. and Jill K. Krisky. "Communications." *Industrial and Labor Relations Review*, vol. 40, no. 1 (1986).

Jarley, Paul and Cheryl L. Maranto. "Union Corporate Campaigns: An Assessment." *Industrial and Labor Relations Review* (July 1990).

Kelly, Ellen P. et al. "NLRB v. Lechmere: Union Quest for Access." *Journal of Labor Research* (Spring 1994).

Kurzman, Dan. "Lovestone's Cold War." *The New Republic*, June 25, 1966.

La Botz, Dan. *Rank and File Rebellion.* New York, Verso, 1990.

Latta, Geoffrey. "Union Organization Among Engineers." *Industrial and Labor Relations Review* (October 1981).

Lens, Sidney. "Lovestone's Diplomacy." *The Nation*, July 6, 1965.

Levitan, Sar A. and Frank Gallo. "Collective Bargaining and Private Sector Professionals." *Monthly Labor Review* (September 1989).

Lynn, Monty L. and Jozell Brister. "Trends in Union Organizing Issues and Tactics." *Industrial Relations* (Winter 1990).

Masters, Marick F. and John Thomas Delaney. "Union Political Activities: A Review of the Empirical Literature." *Industrial and Labor Relations Review* (April 1987).

————. "Union Legislative Records During Reagan's First Term." *Journal of Labor Research* (Winter 1987).

Northrup, Herbert R. "The Rise and Decline of PATCO." *Industrial and Labor Relations Review*, vol. 37, no. 2 (1984).

Northrup, Herbert R., Theresa Diss Greis, and Kay Dowgun. "The Office and Employees International Union." *Journal of Labor Research* (Winter 1988).

Robinson, Archie. *George Meany and His Times.* New York: Simon and Schuster, (1981).

Schur, Lisa and Douglas L. Cruse. "Gender Differences in Attitudes Toward Unions." *Industrial and Labor Relations Review* (October 1992).

Service Employees International Union. *Official Proceedings of the 1993 Convention.*

Sloane, Arthur A. *Hoffa.* Cambridge, MA: MIT Press, 1991.

Strauss, George et al. *The State of the Unions.* Madison, WI: Industrial Relations Research Association, 1990.

Teamsters, International Brotherhood of. *Proceedings of the 1991 Convention.*

United Automobile Workers. *Proceedings of the 1967, 1968, and 1969 Conventions.*

United Food and Commercial Workers. *Proceedings of the 1993 Convention.*

United States Senate. *Interim and Final Reports of the Select Committee on Improper Activities in the Labor or Management Field.* 1958, 1960.

United Steelworkers of America. *Proceedings of the 1990 Convention.*

Voos, Paula B. "Trends in Union Organizing Expenditures, 1953–1977." *Industrial and Labor Relations Review* (October 1984).

Windmuller, John P. "International Unionism in Eclipse." *Industrial and Labor Relations Review* (July 1970).

Zax, Jeffrey S. and Casy Ichniowsky. "Bargaining Laws and Unionization in the Local Public Sector." *Industrial and Labor Relations Review* (April 1990).

Index

About the Author

WALTER GALENSON is Jacob Gould Schurman Professor Emeritus at Cornell University. He was founder and first director of the Center for Chinese Studies at the University of California, Berkeley, founder of the World Employment Program of the International Labor Office, and is past-president of the Association for Comparative Economic Studies. Dr. Galenson is the author of many books, including *Labor and Economic Growth in Five Asian Countries: South Korea, Malaysia, Taiwan, Thailand, and the Philippines* (Praeger, 1992) and *Trade Union Growth and Decline: An International Study* (Praeger, 1994).

ISBN 0-313-29677-4

90000>

EAN

9 780313 296772

HARDCOVER BAR CODE